DIGGING FOR LIFE

4 Years A Slave

ADIANG ASSUOE

DIGGING FOR LIFE

Copyright © 2024 **Adiang Assuoe**

Book publishing services by Opulent Books:

www.OpulentBooks.net

All rights reserved. No part of the book may be reproduced, stored in a retrieval system, or transmitted, in any form or by any means, electronic, mechanical, photocopying, recording, or otherwise, without the prior written permission of the publisher. The only exception is brief quotations in book reviews.

First Printing, 2024

Scripture quotes are taken from the KING JAMES VERSION (KJV): KING JAMES VERSION, public domain.

ISBN: 978-1-916691-17-9

Endorsements

I first met the student I knew as Adiang Assuoe when he attended the New York Film Academy. Over time, he shared with me elements of his amazing life story. But it is only now, through *"Digging for Life"*, that I discovered just how incredible his story is. From Cameroon and Brazil, to America and now the world, Adiang's success might be termed a miracle. But this "miracle" is very much the product of his own talent, determination and ceaseless hard work.

Bill Einreinhofer
Chair Emeritus,
NYFA Broadcast Journalism Department, U.S.A.

I discovered Adiang Assuoe during the 19th edition of the Pan-African Film Festival, which took place in Cannes in October 2023, where I served as a jury member. The short film *"Digging for Life,"* portraying the true story of Adiang, clinched an award in its category. Like many in the audience, *"Digging for Life"* deeply resonated with me, prompting a strong desire to learn more about the actor who portrayed himself in the film.

As a social worker and educator in Nice, France, at a transitional shelter for young Unaccompanied Migrants (UMAs), I frequently encounter teenagers arriving alone, much like ADIANG once did, leaving behind family and friends in pursuit of a better life in a more promising environment.

Self-esteem is the value that one discovers through the eyes of others. "One hundred words to be an educator" – Philippe Gaberan – Editions Erès.

It was imperative for me to reach out to Adiang because, in my perception, he embodied the example of a successful unaccompanied minor (MNA). He transformed a life marked by hardship and various challenges, an immensely arduous journey, into a daily existence of which he can rightfully be proud today, achieved through endurance, a strong work ethic, and faith.

My aim was to connect him with the young individuals under our care, allowing him to become their inspirational figure, the well-suited individual to convey the message: "Believe in yourself, you will thrive!"

The meeting took place on Sunday, October 1, 2023. Assembled in the activity room, I initially recounted Adiang's migrant journey from the day he departed his native Cameroon many years ago. Subsequently, we screened *"Digging for Life."* The profound silence that accompanied the 14-minute viewing and the teary eyes of some mirrored the poignant emotions stirred by the images. To conclude, Adiang engaged in an extensive conversation via WhatsApp with the youths, who eagerly awaited and unanimously expressed, "Adiang, we are grateful for your availability and for your profound words."

Théodora Penda
Social Worker & Educator, France

Never let anyone define who you are. Never let anyone tell you what to do. Be the author of your story; you never know how much people can be inspired by your story. Adiang Assuoe, the time has finally come for the world to understand why so many African young men and women, due to circumstances beyond their control, embrace life in a rather different way. I am particularly overwhelmed by your story after watching *"Digging for Life."* Your courage and faith in God and yourself have today shown us the great personality embodied inside you, and I can only wish you the very best in this life. This is a more than inspiring write-up, and I have learned so much being your friend.

Samy Diko
Cameroonian Artist & Singer, France

"Digging for Life" is a heartfelt story from Adiang, who embodies the essence of resilience and character. His life journey, rife with both triumphs and trials, has made him into the remarkable man he is today. It has been an absolute

honor and privilege to collaborate with Adiang. His story, one full of transparency and authenticity, possesses the potential to profoundly impact countless lives and ignite a flame of inspiration among generations to come. I endorse this book, which is destined to be more than just words on paper but a catalyst for transformative change.

Joe Benjamin
Author & Publisher, U.K.

"Digging for Life" by my childhood friend is a story that describes our home city of Limbe (formerly Victoria) as only Adiang can. It gives you back the childhood stories and memories that we thought lost but, more importantly, reveals where his drive and determination to seek a better outcome for himself and family comes from. The story of his passage of his time into slavery in Angola is gut-wrenching, traumatic, and at times angering. But above all, it exhibits the triumph of the human spirit against all odds and an unshakable belief in God.

Enone Eric Paxton
Friend, U.S.A.

I like to think that it was a reunion, but for my statement to be better understood, I'll start like this: I met my friend Adiang for the first time at an airport. We had been hired to star in a big theater show in my country (Brazil), and we were on the same flight. As soon as we started talking, we felt like two good old friends. When we arrived at our destination, it was no surprise that we shared the same accommodation, as we have a great affinity. Later, I discovered that he had participated in major works in cinema and on one of the main TV channels (Rede Globo). Interestingly, we were also, without knowing it, in the same television series but in different episodes. As time went by, we had some meetings, sometimes about work, sometimes for relaxation. Adiang is a charismatic, authentic, friendly, and true soul. It is a privilege to have him as a friend.

Roger Hal
Friend, Brazil

The time to tell the story is here! Adiang, a dreamer, a visionary, eccentric in all ways, has lived many lives. The simple life of a kid in Africa who decides to follow his dreams collides with the dark and murky world of diamond smugglers, drug dealers, and human traffickers. Riveting! A story of adventure, suffering, worry, but above all, resilience is what Adiang narrates here. Triumph is the light at the end of the tunnel which we hope to see with this narrative. You would love the riveting and compelling story of a young African full of intrigue and adventure who sets out to just follow his dreams.

Flavious Ferim
Friend and classmate Pharmacist, U.S.A.

Dedication

**In Memory of My Mom & Dad
My Senior Brother Jean Claude.**

Though absent at your passing, your love and support have shaped my journey.

To all those facing the horrors of war, enduring trials and tribulations, know that as long as we breathe, there is hope. There is light at the end of the darkest tunnels. Never surrender.

This book is dedicated to the victims, the displaced families, the children, and the mothers of the ANGLOPHONE CRISES (AMBAZONIA WAR) in Cameroon

Adiang and his parents.

30% of the proceeds from each book sold shall be dedicated to our NGO, "DIGGING FOR LIFE." Its sole purpose will be to extend our helping hand to the war victims, offering them a ray of hope amidst despair.

Together, we shall craft a resounding theme, an anthem of solidarity, for this noble cause.

A Message to My Daughters:

To my daughters, Dielle and Endale…

Never forget how much I love you. As you grow older, you will face many challenges in life. Just do your best. Life isn't about waiting for the storm to pass; it's all about learning how to dance in the rain. Every day may not be good, and not all that glitters is gold, but find something good in every day. Laugh, love, live.

Follow your dreams, believe in yourself, and always remember to be awesome. I'll always be with you. I'll always love you…

Adiang…

Contents

Endorsements..iii

Dedication viii

A Message to My Daughters:.......................................ix

Acknowledgments xi

Foreword..xii

Introduction.. xv

Part 1 LIFE IN CAMEROON.............................. 1

1 Childhood in Limbe...3

2 Dreams and Aspiration 25

3 The Music Event 35

4 An Encounter with Mike Tyson..........................49

5 Christian Upbringing..59

Part 2 TRIALS AND TRIBULATIONS 67

6 A Quest for Greatness...69

7 Tragedy Strikes 73

8 Sold into Slavery 79

9 The Diamond Fields of Angola 85

10 The Digging for Life Paradigm..........................97

Part 3 ESCAPE AND REDEMPTION 109

11 A Divine Intervention 111

12 The Long Road to Recovery 125

13 A New Beginning in Brazil 131

14 Giving Back...143

About the Author..149

Acknowledgments

I want to express my deep appreciation to everyone who contributed to this journey. To my family, friends, mentors, editors, and readers—you've played a vital role in bringing this book to life. Your support, encouragement, and belief in me have been my driving force. Thank you for being a part of this incredible adventure.

Foreword

When Adiang Assuoe first unraveled the tapestry of his past as a survivor of slavery, the weight of his words sank into my soul. The chasm between the friend I had come to know and the harrowing path he had walked seemed insurmountable, a stark testament to the depths of human endurance and the scars that linger long after the chains have been shattered.

As his story unfolded, the tremors of pain and resilience beneath his words echoed across the expanse of our shared existence. The chasms that divided our realities deepened, marked by the imprints of history's injustices.

And then, amidst the labyrinthine corridors of his journey, an idea germinated, a purpose that would channel the raw essence of his trauma into a medium that transcended mere recounting—a film that could illuminate the shadows cast by systemic oppression, a canvas to give voice to the countless souls ensnared by chains invisible to the uninitiated eye.

With the shared conviction that the untold stories held within the scars of survivors like Adiang could move mountains, we embarked on an endeavor that merged our worlds and perspectives—a marriage of his lived experience and my cinematic craft. It was a partnership born of empathy, a conscious decision to harness the power of storytelling not as a passive observer but as an active participant in the struggle for justice.

Adiang's narrative unfolded against a backdrop of contrasts as sharp as the blades of historical memory. His journey, one marked by the darkness of slavery, stood in stark relief against my own heritage, tainted by the colonial transgressions of my ancestors in Angola—a reminder that the echoes of oppression still reverberated through generations.

In the realm of filmmaking, where frames capture not just images but emotions, we saw the potential for transformation. We were determined to transcend the limitations of conventional storytelling, to give Adiang agency in the portrayal of his own narrative. With a shared vision, we ventured forth, fusing his authenticity and my technical prowess to bring his experiences to life on the silver screen.

Yet, our aspirations stretched beyond mere documentation. We believed that art, in its most potent form, could be the catalyst for change—a force that could dismantle the walls of indifference and ignite a fire of advocacy for human rights. Adiang's resolute declaration resonated as a beacon of hope: "It's time to tell the story, it's time to tell the world."

As the camera rolled and frames captured the essence of Adiang's journey, we embarked on a mission to translate trauma into triumph, pain into power. Our collaborative efforts, infused with the sweat and tears of shared purpose, sought to bridge the chasm between past and present, the lived and the forgotten, the oppressor and the oppressed.

In the pages that follow, you'll bear witness to a journey that transcends mere storytelling—a journey that, we fervently believe, can catalyze the change we yearn for. Through cinematic alchemy, we endeavor to weave a narrative of hope, to illuminate the resilience etched within the scars of history, and to amplify the voices that have long been stifled by silence.

This is the chronicle of our collective commitment, a testimony to the potential of art to shape destinies, to rewrite narratives, and to redefine the boundaries of human compassion. This is a testament to the power of collaboration and the indomitable spirit of those who rise from the ashes of adversity, demanding to be heard. This is the story that, with every frame and every word, we strive to tell—the story that demands to be told.

Foreword by:

JOÃO QUEIROGA

A friend and Director of the Documentary "Digging for Life." Former professor at the New York Film Academy where he was Adiang's teacher. He is now teaching at Northwestern University in Doha, Qatar.

Introduction

This is the story of an unusual man, a man who ventured through trials and tribulations to bring a slice of heaven into his family's life. Before delving into this narrative, there's a profound message worth considering:

There is no one quite like you. There has never been anyone quite like you. There shall never be anyone quite like you. Therefore, know yourself. Be yourself. Authenticity is everything.

I embarked on the journey of writing this book after an extended period of profound solitude and contemplation. During these introspective moments, I recalled a valuable piece of advice: "Speak not merely to share your thoughts but to enhance the well-being of others. Speak to alleviate their circumstances, for in doing so, you will discern the distinction between speaking truth and embodying love itself. Love always takes into account the consequences." It is this principle that has led me to pen these words, as they are the medium through which I can share the lessons of my life with all of you.

You see, passing judgment upon an individual does not reveal their true essence; instead, it reflects who we are. This is especially true when our judgments are clouded by anger, jealousy, negativity, and unfulfilled desires. In life, what we perceive when observing others hinges on the clarity of the window through which we view them.

Let me refer to a story about the Buddha, who, when asked by a young monk why bad things happen to good people, offered this profound insight:

"If one has faith, all things have meaning." He continued: "I asked for strength, and God gave me difficulties to make me strong" (Biblical Joseph). "I asked for wisdom, and God gave me problems to solve" (Biblical King Solomon). "I asked for courage, and God gave me dangers to overcome" (Biblical King David). "I asked for love, and God gave me troubled people to help" (Biblical Moses). My prayers were answered.

Here's food for thought:

"We should all bear in mind that the greatest glory in life lies not in never falling, but in rising every time you fall." A person who has never experienced misery would never know the wisdom that comes with it. Don't be afraid of loneliness because at least you know you're with someone you have confidence in, and that is yourself. No one can stop you from becoming great but yourself, so never be afraid of loneliness; lions walk alone. In loneliness, you discover the real you.

Trees don't hang around with the grass, even though they all started from the same place. Choose your friends wisely.

Fight to get what you like; otherwise, you'll be forced to like what you get.

You can't find happiness except by giving happiness.

It's not the desire to win that makes you a winner, but the refusal to lose.

Respect failure as much as you respect success. Advice from people with scars is a life lesson.

Pain shall leave you only when it has taught you a lesson.

Words have no value when actions are opposite.

When you live to achieve a high goal, hard work is not an option; it is a necessity.

A rich man digs to find gold, while a poor man complains about the price of the spade.

The Bible says, "As long as the earth remains, there will be a harvest; there will be good and bad times." To everything, there is a season; it's like saying nothing lasts forever. If you're broke right now, that's just a season—it cannot last forever. Wealth is on the way. And if you are rich and wealthy right now, you must use that wealth strategically and properly because that wealth may be challenged at any time, as everything is for a season. If you're in a pit right now, life is on the way. If you are in pain, health is on the way. If you are abandoned, a company is coming to meet you. Nothing remains forever, and no condition is permanent. The key to success is outlasting the season, remaining steady until the season passes, whether it's a season of good times or bad times.

The first step will not take you where you want to go in life, but it takes you out of where you were. Live for what tomorrow has to offer rather than dwelling on what yesterday took away from you.

To avoid correcting a mistake is a mistake.

Don't allow the pressure of those who consume their harvest to make you eat your sowing seed.

Some people will never congratulate you because you've grown beyond the limitations they had placed on you. The size of God depends on the distance between you and Him. The closer you are to Him, the greater His presence in your life. How close are you to God?

Adiang understood why his life meant so much to his family, especially his loving mother, Nyanti. As he now understands, we are all chosen and called to various duties. His journey is unique, and he must be fully prepared for this purpose. The difficulties he endured were nothing but steps on the path to the platform of excellence that the Lord had prepared for him.

Can you now tell me why you are stagnant in life? What's so bad that you have done that God can't use you?

Abraham was a liar. Noah was an alcoholic. Job doubted God several times. Samson was promiscuous. David was a sinner and a murderer. Elijah battled suicidal thoughts. Peter was embarrassed to acknowledge his association with Jesus. Rahab was a prostitute. The disciples were often weak, jealous of each other, and even fell asleep when Jesus was arrested. The Samaritan woman couldn't maintain her marriage. Moses wrestled with anxiety. Moses wrestled with anxiety and was a stutterer.

Again, what's so bad that you have done that God can't use you?

Never be ashamed of your past, your present situation, or your battles. Fight all your battles with dignity. You're not the first nor the last to go through embarrassment, financial struggles, or health challenges. There is absolutely nothing happening to you that is entirely unique. The Bible tells us stories of men and women who endured severe afflictions before emerging victorious. As Romans 15:4 reminds us, "For whatsoever things were written aforetime were written for our learning, that we through patience and comfort of the scriptures might have hope."

Hope to rise again. Hope to become a better person. Hope that your ministry will flourish once more. Hope that you will have the last laugh.

The manifestation of victory encompasses both the positive and negative experiences we all face in life. I encourage you to embrace loneliness because when you decide to be true to yourself, you may find yourself on a solitary path. Loneliness often accompanies the pursuit of uniqueness and purpose. It is in this solitude that you discover your true self and your potential to change the world.

As Romans 8:18 assures us, "For I reckon that the sufferings of this present time are not worthy to be compared with the glory which shall be revealed in us."

Someone once said, "We already will lose everything we have to lose. We are all in this game, and there's no escape except by death." As no one will get out of this life but through death, whether you want it or not. With that being said, I think there's nothing more practical than developing a vision. Without a vision, we are chaotic, fragmented, hopeless, and disappointed. Someone can stop you just by putting up a single obstacle. Your house is divided amongst itself, and you have no forward movement. You're not enthusiastic, and your life is a sequence of frustrations and tragedies. That is not what you are called to be. You're called to be a visionary constructor of the paradisal vision.

I sincerely hope to touch as many people, irrespective of their positions in life, to understand that there is a reward for our constructive and positive contributions to make this world a better place for us and the future. You can certainly be whatever you wish to be as long as you truly believe and go for it; otherwise, it's just a dream, just a wish. I sincerely wish and hope you understand the meaning of living up to your potential in this life and living it truly because only when you get it right can you be truly satisfied. You shall know when it's right.

One thing is certain: if you stick to the Word, you'll come back with a testimony. What God wants to give you in your life is not just healing, a job, or money, but His Word in your spirit. It will make you into what it talks about.

You are shining by the power of the Holy Ghost; it is your season, it is your time. Nothing can stop or hinder you. This is your time, this is your hour. Favor is yours.

Whatever you are looking for, remember that being broke is part of the game; staying broke is your choice. Believe you've got it, and it shall be yours. Believe me, this is a personal, true-life story. Nobody but you can tell it just the way it is because not only to inspire but to help you achieve your dreams. I want us all to impact the world and leave behind us what Christ meant when He said we could do greater things if we believe.

Remember, every morning you have two choices: either continue to sleep with your dreams or wake up and chase them. You can't quit now; you've come a long way. Be proud of yourself; you've made it through all the bad days. I know you've got a lot going on, but you're stronger than you think. If there's one thing you can do, it's to change tomorrow. You've got to be better than you were today, and don't forget, the future depends on you to be excellent, so don't stay in the past. You'll be alright; I know you will. I'm proud of you.

"Money is the root of all evil." The one-liner that has many of us in bondage. Almost everything we ever learned about success our whole life is a lie because if it wasn't, everybody

should be successful and financially free. Teach yourself out of the way you were taught to be successful. The reason you think being successful is hard is because of the way you were taught how to do it. The keys to the kingdom of God are truth, and bondage is a result of lies. The person we love is the one who told us the lie, and it becomes hard to let go of the lie because we got it from mom or dad, grandma, grandad, or from somebody who loves us, our favorite teacher in school.

So I learned something that wasn't true from somebody I care about and who cared about me, and so, therefore, in order for me to abandon that, I feel like I'm abandoning them. So I am going to hold onto this lie that's keeping me broke and ready to die at any time. You've got to tear down the strongholds established. There's only one reason we protect the lie: it shows we are not abandoning our family, and we lie after getting success because we don't want our family to think evil of our desire to have more money, drive nice cars, and live in nice houses because we are afraid we will be judged by them.

Just like money or being successful, we are only as good as we stay in motion. Remember, no condition is permanent. Teach yourself to flow and not to accumulate money, which is not wealth. Wealth is the ability to create value because the ability to create value creates something more important than the accumulation of money. It creates cash.

In the pages that follow, you will embark on a transformative journey through the wisdom and insights of Adiang's story. As we get into the essence of this book, *"Digging for Life,"* I invite you to unearth the immense power that resides within you.

This journey is not just about Adiang – but also about you discovering the treasures of purpose, vision, and resilience buried within your soul. Life, as we know it, is a quest filled with both challenges and triumphs. It is a journey where we must dig deep to find the meaning, the strength, and the opportunities that lie beneath the surface.

The stories within these pages will remind you that even the greatest heroes and heroines of history faced trials, doubts, and setbacks. They stumbled, fell, and faced their own unique set of obstacles. Yet, they dug deep into their inner reserves and emerged victorious, leaving a legacy that still inspires us today.

"Digging for Life" is an exploration of the human spirit's boundless potential to overcome adversity, embrace vision, and discover a life filled with purpose. It is a call to action for each of us to become visionary constructors of our paradisal visions and to unlock the hidden treasures that await us.

As you turn the pages and immerse yourself in the stories and wisdom that lie ahead, remember that you, too, possess the power to dig deep, unearth your purpose, and forge a path toward a more meaningful and fulfilling life. Let *"Digging for Life"* be your inspiration on this remarkable journey.

Adiang Assuoe

Part 1

LIFE IN CAMEROON

> "Son, never play the same game as them. They count on their families, but your family counts on you. Be very careful. Remember that one day these friends will all go away, and you'll be left alone. The situation at home will remain the same if you forget what family you come from, what type of life your family lives. There are those who succeed with the help of their parents, but you will have to succeed to help your family. You are not fighting the same fight. They were born on the right side of the shore, but you have to throw yourself into the river and face the crocodiles to succeed. Be very careful, son."

— *Nyanti*

1

Childhood in Limbe

Imagine a seaside city nestled in the lush embrace of the South West region of Cameroon, a place where the rhythmic waves of the Atlantic Ocean serenade your senses. Limbe, home to an estimated population of 96,629 souls today, beckons with its enchanting allure—a coastal haven that has captured the hearts of tourists from across the nation and around the globe. Its black sand, a unique gift of nature, sets a dramatic backdrop to the picturesque seashores that stretch as far as the eye can see.

Founded in 1858 by the British Missionary Alfred Saker, Limbe bore the name Victoria in honor of the reigning Queen at the time. Yet, in 1982, a profound transformation occurred. The city, now pulsating with a history as rich and diverse as its people, assumed a new identity—Limbe. This change paid homage to the city's own narrative, one steeped in cultural heritage and ancient stories.

Back in the late '70s and early '80s, Limbe was a quaint town, brimming with cultural diversity and a modest population. A place where Adiang, a local resident, could swear he knew nearly every soul in his neighborhood by name. Little did he know that this close-knit community would soon become a backdrop for a tale of remarkable journeys, shared dreams, and the indomitable spirit of its people.

Moliwe: A Gateway to Limbe

Moliwe stands as the threshold into Limbe, an unassuming marker that signifies the administrative boundary separating two distinct municipalities: Mutengene and Limbe. Nestled in the valley between the undulating terrain of hilly Mutengene and the equally hilly Mile 4, Moliwe plays a unique role in the local geography.

The main road, distinguished by a broad white line down its center, serves as both a lifeline and a tourist attraction for Adiang. Every Saturday morning, he treads along this road's well-trodden path, leading him to the Mandolin Forest at Mile 2. His mission? To collect the firewood his mother, Nyanti, will use to prepare meals for the family throughout the week.

When the road falls silent, Adiang and his brothers seize the moment to dart across it, barefooted. The sensation of the sun-baked asphalt against their soles is unforgettable, an experience uniquely theirs. From the vantage point atop the hill at Mile 4, this road unveils itself like the racetrack of a Formula 1 circuit. Its treacherous curves, the sentinel palm trees lining its sides, the grasslands that rival Argentina's pampas, the level stretches, and occasional vistas of the city cascading down toward the Atlantic Ocean—all of this combines to create a panoramic spectacle that would be a dying man's final wish.

Moliwe, by and large, remains a relatively small town, home to a sizable camp of laborers primarily employed by the Cameroon Development Corporation (CDC). These dedicated workers toil for long hours amidst the palm, banana, rubber, and coffee plantations that envelope the area. As you approach Moliwe on the road to Limbe, the briny aroma of the Atlantic Ocean begins to permeate the air, offering a tantalizing hint of what lies ahead.

Driving through Moliwe, one might be deceived by a sense of abandonment. Most of its residents spend the majority of their days toiling in the plantations. From a distance, it might seem as if nobody resides here except for the children engaged in spirited football matches in front of their modest homes, which more closely resemble huts. Originally, the CDC camps were designed to accommodate individuals who came to the city as laborers in the plantations you see, but as time marched on, families sprouted within these cramped quarters.

Departing Moliwe and entering Mile 4, the gateway to Limbe, one is greeted by the vision of Mile 4 perched atop the hill, nestled at the foot of Mount Cameroon and adjacent to the Bojongo hill. Mile 4, in essence, represents a sloping facet of the city—a place that marks the starting point for the annual cross-country race and city mini-marathon, culminating at the Limbe Community Field.

Words can scarcely do justice to the breathtaking panorama that unfolds while descending the hill toward the heart of the city. The pristine white stripe dividing the unique asphalt road signifies the transition point for vehicles entering and leaving Limbe. On both sides of this road, lush palm trees thrive. When ready, these trees yield the nuts that are harvested to produce the palm oil cherished both within Cameroon and abroad. Even after their felling, these palms continue to offer their bounty, providing the finest traditional palm wine, known as Matango.

Passing through Mile 2 and descending toward Limbe, a substantial cemented crossover bridge comes into view, adorned with a sign that warmly beckons: "WELCOME TO LIMBE..."

As you embark on your descent into the heart of Limbe, an enthralling journey awaits, filled with captivating sights and experiences that define this vibrant city.

Mile 2, an integral part of Limbe, is home to two prominent educational institutions, the newly erected Lycee Classique GHS (Government High School) Limbe and its neighbor, the Government Bilingual Secondary School Limbe. These institutions symbolize the city's commitment to education.

Mile 2 is closely connected to Mile 1, forming a seamless transition as you journey downhill. The Mile 2 bridge marks this transition, spanning over one of the branches of the Limbe River. Adjacent to the bridge, you'll find the Government Primary School and Ecole Francophone Mile 1, a testament to the city's dedication to nurturing young minds. As you delve deeper into Limbe, you'll encounter the imposing edifice of the city's pride—the General and Public Hospital, inaugurated by the former President Amadou Ahidjo, affectionately known as the "Mile 1 Hospital."

Continuing your descent, you'll be drawn to the kaleidoscope of color adorning the numerous carabot (plank) houses that line the roadside. These vibrant facades beckon, providing a stark contrast to the lush greenery of the surrounding mbende and cassava farms. As you approach the junction, you'll encounter Half Mile, where Mayor Mrs. Meboke has introduced a modern marvel—traffic lights—an essential addition for managing the city's burgeoning population and vehicular traffic.

On the left-hand side, the journey remains equally enchanting. Descending the hill, you'll come face-to-face with the Bahai Church edifice at Mile 2, a testament to Limbe's diverse religious landscape. Nearby stands the National Comprehensive Secondary School, a formidable contender against GHS Limbe in the yearly school games and competitions. With its large, yellow-painted classroom walls and extensive football field, this institution fosters both academics and athletics. Next in line is the National Water Corporation (SNEC), surrounded by the residences of the neighborhood.

As you continue your descent toward Half Mile, the view of Mr. (Paa) Salle's unfinished and abandoned building emerges, a silent witness to the passage of time. Your journey leads you to the Mothercare Supermarket, and further down the hill lies Mr. (Paa) Menchops' multifaceted buildings, nestled at the Cassava Farms junction.

Crossing this junction, you'll encounter the multifunctional Presbyterian Youth Center, affectionately known as PYC. This center serves not only as a commercial secondary school but also as a kindergarten for the youngest members of the community and a lively dancehall during Christmas festivities. Adjacent to PYC stands the renowned Donangu Pharmacy, with the Total gas filling station just a stone's throw away. This intersection, known as Half Mile, serves as a pivotal point within the city.

Half Mile represents a square four-corner junction that delineates the neighborhoods of Gardens, Church Street, Mile One, and the continuation of the main road leading to Downbeach. It's an intersection that leads to diverse experiences.

Let's start with Church Street—a name that belies its eclectic character. Far from being a holy sanctuary, this street has grown to be a hub of promiscuity, gang culture, and devout Christians—all coexisting within its bounds. Situated on the left-hand side of the four-corner junction at Half Mile, it's flanked by the Total gas filling station and the adjacent Boulangerie. The infamous Crazy Horse Dancing Club stands as a gateway to Church Street, known for its cheap entertainment and clientele that includes low-profile gangsters known as "Broke Enters." As you ascend the hill, you'll pass eerie-looking carabot, plank, zinc, and brick houses, setting the stage for what lies ahead.

The renowned Namondo Bar, a weathered blue-painted carabot house where beer crates double as chairs, serves as a meeting point for the city's youth. Across the street, you'll find Country Man's Beer Wholesale Store, which earned its proprietor a ticket to the World Cup in Spain for breaking records as the highest alcohol wholesaler and distributor in the city—satisfying the ever-thirsty population's needs.

Further along this street is the Sea Palace, a four-story building owned by the notorious Paa Mukala. It's a place where girls of all ages, known as "Nkane," seek potential customers for nocturnal adventures. Ironically adjacent to the world of sensual indulgence stands the Apostolic Church—an invitation to repentance amidst the temptations.

Within this particular part of town lies Madame Weleji's Beautiful Holiday Inn Hotel, nestled in the Lump Sum quarter, amidst a neighborhood that poses challenging road access. The Catholic Church, majestically perched atop the hill, symbolizes a journey of rebirth and spiritual awakening.

Half Mile serves as a crucial beltway that separates the neighborhoods of Gardens and New Town, situated on both the east and west sides of the city. These neighborhoods eventually converge at the shores of the Atlantic Ocean in Downbeach, the southernmost part of Limbe.

Top of Form

As you wander through the streets of Limbe, formerly known as Victoria, you'll be struck by the unconventional and captivating architecture that characterizes most of its houses. Limbe's urban landscape seems to defy traditional town planning, creating an almost desolate yet strangely alluring atmosphere. It's a place where organized chaos meets the beauty of spontaneity. In some ways, it might remind you of Brazil's iconic favelas, or ghettoes.

One remarkable example of this vibrant chaos is the neighborhood of Gardens, which mirrors the intricate maze of Brazil's favelas, complete with shortcuts leading to different corners of the city. Within minutes, you can navigate through these alleys and find yourself in the southernmost part of Limbe, known as Bota—a journey that would normally take an hour.

Gardens begins its narrative with the BATA supermarket, conveniently located just after the Texaco gas filling station at the Half Mile junction. Opposite this supermarket, you'll encounter the Boyo Bar spot, marking the beginning of a bustling stretch of road lined with small retail stores and businesses. The Apollo photo studio, situated near the Youth and Sports Divisional head office, serves as a pivotal junction connecting the eastern and western parts of Gardens.

As you continue along the main road, you'll embark on a winding journey that leads you to the Cassava Farms. This path eventually ascends the hills, taking you back to Mile One.

This circuitous route underscores the connection between Gardens and Brazil's favelas.

On the western side, Gardens descends directly toward the Limbe River, known locally as Njembe Water, which serves as a natural boundary separating the neighborhood from the Botanical Gardens—an iconic tourist destination. Gardens also boasts the picturesque Coconut Island, a hilly enclave adorned with tall coconut trees surrounded by a charming collection of zinc, carabot, and a few brick houses. This idyllic spot is primarily inhabited by expatriate families from diverse backgrounds, adding to the neighborhood's cultural richness. This hilly piece of land within the gardens stands out due to its unique characteristics. Almost as beautiful as the Green Mountain in Muscat City of the Arab Republic of Oman.

Coconut Island is linked to the mainland by the main road leading to Downbeach to the north, while the southern boundary is formed by Gardens' main road, leading to the Limbe River. To the west, an extension of the island merges with Gardens itself, and to the east lies the Community field, a hub for cultural and provincial events.

Gardens' charm extends to the Centenary Stadium, where football matches unfold. Among its prominent clubs are Victoria United, an elite team, and its formidable rival, Elecsport of Limbe, owned by the SONEL National Electricity Company. Other notable clubs include Camark Limbe, owned by the National Producing Marketing Board, which primarily focuses on cocoa and coffee farming, and the SONARA football club, owned by the national refinery and renowned as the wealthiest club in town.

Gardens stretches to various junctions, including Limbe Camp, Middle Farms, Cite Nanga, and Sokolo, which is considered an outskirts neighborhood that extends to the far ends of Batoke. This journey takes you through the National Refinery SONARA, Ngeme, Bota Island, Idenau, and Debuncha—a city that holds the distinction of being the second wettest in the world.

Going to school when the sea overflows into the mainland, he improvised ways to reach the classroom.

Within the heart of Gardens, you'll find the unique Police and Gendarmerie stations, strategically located near the Customs office and the Treasury headquarters—an essential safeguard for the city's financial security against armed robberies.

During Adiang's youth, he and his friends frequently visited the Botanical Garden to savor the assortment of fruits it offered. The initiative "Keep Limbe Clean Every First Wednesday of the Month" earned the city recognition as the second cleanest in the nation. Residents actively participated in cleaning the city by cutting overgrown grass along the roadside, clearing gutters, and enhancing the aesthetics of houses near the main road. In school, pupils divided their tasks, with some cleaning teachers' houses and others focusing on school grounds.

Childhood days were filled with activities like football, table tennis, dodgeball, and marbles—daily rituals in Adiang's life. Football, in particular, became an indispensable part of their routine, offering an escape from household chores as they joined friends for spirited matches. Football fields were scattered throughout the area, and when one was absent, they'd create their own. Swimming, often in nearby rivers, became a cherished pastime, especially after school and on weekends. Yet, whenever tragedy struck—a drowning or an untimely death—the group would relocate to a new river, attributing the misfortune to witches in the former one, deeming it a sacrifice to the Queen of the Ocean, known as Mami Wata.

The Botanical Garden, a gift from the Queen of England, houses an herbarium of diverse plant species, providing a refreshing oasis for youth seeking to savor the fruits of nature's bounty.

Discovering Downbeach and Coastal Delights

Jungle Village, a cultural relic reminiscent of the Roman Colosseum, once witnessed great warriors testing their mettle in the arena during pala pala (fighting) sports events in the

1960s. Today, it is transformed into the epicenter of cultural dance competitions, a hub of vibrant activity, as Limbe's youth vie for qualifications in preparation for Youth Day, celebrated every 11th of February. The village's transformation mirrors the evolution of Limbe itself, embracing its cultural heritage while adapting to contemporary rhythms.

Just beyond Jungle Village lies the Limbe Wildlife Center, also known as the Zoo. This sanctuary rescues and rehabilitates a diverse range of wildlife, including lowland gorillas, monkeys, crocodiles, giraffes, and lions. It has become a renowned tourist attraction, drawing visitors from far and wide.

Leaving Half Mile and journeying towards Downbeach, you'll encounter a three-headed fork in the road. To the left, a road begins at the Agip gas station, leading through the motor park, a bustling hub where you can catch buses connecting to various parts of the nation. Continuing straight, beyond the Rainbow Pharmacy, you'll arrive at a roundabout. This intersection offers three distinct routes, all leading to Downbeach.

The leftward path guides you past the Black and White nightclub, Bay Hotel, the Presbyterian Boys' Primary School, and the church. As you reach the end of this route, you'll find the Land and Survey Labogenie headquarters.

In the middle of this trident-like intersection lies Motto Spare Parts Stores, primarily owned by the Igbo people from Nigeria, affectionately known as SAPA Road. This road leads directly to the Sonel National Electricity headquarters, with the BEAC Central African States Bank situated immediately behind Sonel.

To the right, you'll encounter the NOBRA beer warehouse (Nouvelle Brasseries), adjacent to Doctor Tchwenko's clinic. This route leads you across the Jembe River. Here, you'll find Paa Tita's Pressbook printing press, located opposite the Presbyterian Girls Primary School. Additionally, a cluster of financial institutions and banks, including BICIC and BIAO, can be found in this area.

Opposite the Senior Divisional Office, just beside the monument and statue of Alfred Saker, the city's founder, you'll find the Victoria Club—a favored beer spot among the city's elite.

As the road stretches ahead, you'll enter Mbonjo. You can't avoid a pause to admire the beautiful edifice of the Chamber of Commerce with the most spectacular balcony view of the Atlantic Ocean. Mbonjo is a neighborhood mainly inhabited by fishermen from Ghana, Togo, and Benin Republic. The same route leads to Man O' War Bay, a military camp for soldiers and their families.

Childhood soccer days.

The Atlantic Beach Hotel and Miramar Hotel, both uniquely positioned near the ocean, offer breathtaking views of the Atlantic. However, nothing compares to the majestic structure of the Senior Divisional Officer's Residence, perched atop a hill, providing an unparalleled vantage point in the city.

During their adventures along the beach shores, the children eagerly search for fallen coconuts from the numerous coconut trees that dot the landscape. The reward is sometimes finding these fruits, which they skillfully open using sea rocks, peel with bare hands, and crack open the dried nuts, which typically contain no water. However, there's a humorous caveat to indulging in these seaside coconuts: one must exercise caution not to release gas in crowded areas. An embarrassing incident in the classroom serves as a memorable lesson, as Adiang stealthily lifted one side of his buttock to release gas, causing a commotion that led to the evacuation of the entire class due to the noxious odor. It was an experience that led him to give up eating sea coconuts from that day forward.

The Guavas and a Close Call

Another lesson from Adiang's adventurous childhood was learned within the Botanical Garden, amidst a grove of guava trees. He had never encountered such plump, ripe, and sweet guavas before, and he devoured them with the fervor of a wild animal. Consequently, he skipped dinner that evening due to the sheer volume of guavas filling his stomach. Little did he know that this indulgence would lead to an uncomfortable and embarrassing ordeal.

The following day, Adiang rushed to the toilet, desperately needing to relieve himself. However, his anus could not bear the pain inflicted by the dry guava seeds he had consumed. In his distress, he sought assistance from his ever-resourceful mother, Nyanti. What ensued was a rather unconventional but necessary procedure, conducted right on the veranda in full view of the entire neighborhood.

Nyanti initiated a local remedy by concocting a mixture of hot cocoa, soap, and water, which she promptly administered into Adiang's exposed anus. Within seconds, the guavas in his stomach reacted as if a dam had burst, causing an explosive release of guava-laden contents. Adiang endured this rather humiliating experience for nearly an hour, with friends and neighbors looking on and erupting in laughter. Needless to say, this incident left an indelible mark, ensuring that Adiang would never again partake in the consumption of guavas.

However, this was not the only close call Adiang faced during his childhood. On a sunny afternoon, while playfully engaging with his uncle, a precarious situation unfolded. His uncle, holding Adiang by the legs with his head facing downward, began spinning around rapidly. The centrifugal force grew so intense that Adiang became dizzy and disoriented. Tragically, his uncle lost his grip, sending Adiang hurtling through the house until he crash-landed with his skull impacting the unyielding cement floor. Both uncle and nephew lay unconscious.

The noise of their fall alerted the neighbors, who rushed to the scene and discovered a badly disfigured child with a pronounced forehead injury from the impact with the unforgiving floor. Adiang was swiftly transported to the hospital, where he remained unconscious for several hours. His road to recovery involved nearly a month of receiving frontal head massages to alleviate the trauma. This harrowing incident served as a stark reminder of the fragility of life and the unpredictable nature of childhood adventures.

Simple Joys and Festive Days

His childhood was marked by a captivating blend of simplicity and accessibility. Life was uncomplicated, and everything we needed was within reach. Movement was a breeze, as they rarely had the means to afford taxi fares, nor did they particularly require them. With shortcuts scattered throughout the city, the kids, believed they could often reach destinations faster than the taxis could. It was a time of carefree exploration and endless possibilities.

From Monday to Friday, lives revolved around school, commencing at 7 a.m. and concluding at 2 p.m. Saturdays were dedicated to assisting parents with farming activities. They helped gather firewood for weekday cooking, worked alongside mothers in tending to cornfields, vegetable patches, and fruit orchards. Later in the day, the soccer fields beckoned, providing endless hours of football matches on the numerous playgrounds scattered across the city. The lengths they traveled to watch or partake in these games were nothing short of astounding, just as the adventures to various rivers held their own sense of thrill and excitement.

Sundays were designated for mandatory church attendance. While adults congregated for services across various denominations, children filled the Sunday school halls, eagerly absorbing the lessons and stories imparted to them.

The 11th of February and the 20th of May held special significance as Youth Day and National Day, respectively. Parents would purchase new uniforms and canvas shoes for their children, as schools encouraged a polished appearance to vie for cash prizes during these festivities. On the 20th of May, Dad received a well-deserved medal of honor for his dedicated decade of service at the Chamber of Commerce. The occasion was marked by a lively celebration at home, complete with an abundance of libations and delectable cuisine.

During these festive times, akin to Christmas and New Year's Day, the youth dancing clubs at the PYC (Presbyterian Youth Center) in Half Mile opened their doors to young revelers. For some, these celebrations served as the initiatory steps into less wholesome lifestyles, leading them down a perilous path.

Summer Ventures and Life Lessons

The Big Holidays stretched across three idyllic months, from July to September. During this time, some ventured to their ancestral villages or explored other cities to visit uncles and aunties. Others embarked on entrepreneurial journeys, engaging in small-scale buying and selling ventures within the neighborhood. For students, holiday classes served as a means of preparation for the upcoming school year.

Nyanti, with her enterprising spirit, led the household into various business ventures. Whether it was selling food at the SONARA construction site or peddling cooked groundnuts (peanuts), avocados, mangoes, and more in trays balanced gracefully on their heads as they traversed the city, Nyanti sought every opportunity to generate income for her family.

Nyanti dishing out food.

One particularly profitable avenue was vending during football games. However, the challenge lay in gaining access to the field while carrying their substantial trays of food. Adiang and his friends devised clever solutions. They would arrive at the games as early as possible, approaching the organizers with cups of peanuts as bribes to gain entry. When they arrived late, they resorted to scaling the walls with their trays of food after stashing their peanuts in sizable plastic bags, or they'd join hands with adults, pretending to be their sons, to secure field access.

Downbeach, however, offered the prospect of more substantial earnings. By joining forces with the Alaja people, primarily hailing from Benin Republic, Ghana, and Ivory Coast (West Africans), and the bolo boys, Adiang and his friends assisted in pushing canoes ashore laden with fish. In return, they received buckets of fish to sell, adding to their earnings.

Opportunities often presented themselves, as the fishermen occasionally became too engrossed in their work, allowing the boys to discreetly collect fish from the nets, hiding their ill-gotten gains in secret buckets. By day's end, all involved were content, and as school resumed, new tennis shoes, uniforms, pencils, books, and more hinted at a seemingly affluent background. Only they knew the truth about their financial sources, eagerly anticipating the next vacation to return to the beach.

Some children chose to forego their education, opting for a life at the beach. Coming from troubled homes, they became permanent bolo boys, earning their keep in the coastal world of fishing.

Adiang playing in the farm, while Nyanti is working.

Another holiday job involved gathering dried coffee and filling bags for export at the National Producing Marketing Board warehouses in Bota and SAPA Road. Adiang's initial experience proved to be a harsh lesson, with grueling work hours from 7 a.m. to 5 p.m., occasionally stretching to 6 p.m. This was far from the carefree days of youth, filled with football games and river swims. It was an experience he couldn't bear, and he chose not to return.

The Master SONARA International tennis competition, organized by the National Refinery with the patronage of the renowned international tennis star Yannick Noah, coincided with classes Yannick Noah provided to the children of SONARA employees. Nyanti decided to send Adiang and his brothers to sell peanuts and bananas at the games. However, Adiang's sense of shame led him to distant neighborhoods to peddle his wares, foregoing the opportunity to participate in the games.

Later in life, Adiang would learn the profound lesson that one should never be ashamed of their background or their parents' circumstances. Hard work and self-belief can propel anyone toward their dreams. Many individuals who had achieved excellence on prestigious platforms were not born into privilege but had forged their paths through determination and dedication.

Awakening to the Reality of Poverty

At the tender ages of 12 and 13, a sobering awareness began to settle upon him – the realization that his family lived in dire financial straits. He sensed the pressing need to alter this stark reality, but given his youth, he found himself limited in what he could do. His role primarily involved assisting Nyanti and obediently following her directives. He placed his hopes and prayers, much like many African families do during Sunday school church services, in the prospect of a miraculous change in their circumstances. Instead of channeling his thoughts, creativity, and effort toward changing their predicament, he placed his faith in divine intervention.

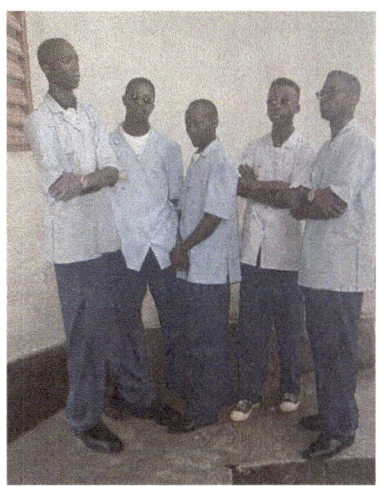

Memories of Lycée Classique GHS Limbe. From left to right: Wacka Eric Jackai, Sanyi Ndive, Adiang Assuoe, Evat and late Teh Roland.

As you might expect, the outcome was as expected – nothing changed. The status quo remained unaltered, persisting for several more years, fueling his frustration. After completing primary school, he grew insistent on attending either Sasse College or Lycee Molyko, recognizing that these institutions produced the nation's prominent figures.

In the arena of school sports, GHS consistently emerged victorious in most disciplines, while PYC excelled in handball, and Comprehensive College and GHS Limbe engaged in thrilling volleyball finals. Adiang's family had originally migrated from the French-speaking regions of Cameroon, fleeing the turmoil of the Maquizard war in Manjo and Nkongsamba. They sought refuge in Limbe, drawn by the promise of better opportunities. Initially, they settled on Coconut Island, which, at the time, was the sole locale where French-speaking Cameroonians could be found. Adiang was born on Coconut Island and raised in Mile One, later relocating to Unity Quarter annex Bakoko.

Born into a family of nine children, all sharing the same parents, Adiang occupied the sixth position among his siblings. His mother had borne twins three times, earning her the endearing title of "magne," while his father was known as "Tagne." Despite the constraints of their financial situation, Adiang enjoyed a richly affectionate childhood. Adored by everyone, especially his parents, he was unhindered in his explorations. As a bright student in the classroom, he harbored dreams of a brighter future for himself and his family. However, he couldn't help but notice the glaring disparities between what he possessed and what his friends enjoyed. It was during these times that he began to engage in frequent dialogues with Nyanti, his mother, about their circumstances.

> "Never regret a day in your life. Good days bring happiness, bad days bring experience, and the worst days bring lessons. The best days bring memories."
>
> – *Nyanti*

2

Dreams and Aspiration

Buea, the vibrant headquarters of the South West Province, stands proudly as the capital city, overseeing the intricate tapestry of administrative offices that govern the entire province. This enchanting region boasts the grandeur of Mount Cameroon, a majestic peak soaring to 4100 meters above sea level. Revered by locals and christened "The Chariot of the Gods" by Portuguese explorers, this volcanic wonder has long been shrouded in myths and tales, often attributed to the mountain's resident deities, affectionately referred to as EPASSA MOTTO.

It is in this captivating city that Adiang embarked on a transformative journey, spending five pivotal years of his life pursuing the dreams that had ignited within him. His destination of choice was none other than the Lycee Bilingue de Molyko, an educational institution of unparalleled prestige, inaugurated with great pomp by President Amadou Ahidjo in 1971.

For Adiang, the Lycee Bilingue de Molyko was not just a school; it was a gateway to a future he envisioned. It was here that he received the gift of education, a precious offering that bestowed upon him the wisdom, knowledge, and clarity of purpose necessary to conquer the world.

As he stepped onto the campus on those initial days, Adiang was greeted by a sight that took his breath away. The Lycee's sprawling grounds boasted towering structures with grand staircases that led to various classrooms, along with state-of-the-art laboratories where aspiring scientists could conduct experiments. It was here, amidst the halls of learning, that he first encountered tales of students beseeching their often-uncomprehending parents for "photosynthesis" to aid in chemistry experiments—a testament to the dedication and enthusiasm that permeated the school.

Accommodations within the Lycee were provided for male students, yet the sheer number of students necessitated alternative arrangements. Many found themselves renting apartments in close proximity to the school or living with welcoming families in the heart of Molyko. Within the Lycee's hallowed halls, teachers not only imparted knowledge but also nurtured their students as if they were their own children. Love and camaraderie filled the campus, fostering an environment in which failure seemed inconceivable.

In these halls of promise, Adiang's journey toward his aspirations began—a journey that would ultimately shape his destiny and set him on a path to realizing his dreams.

Top Student

The traditional stage, standing ovation during results proclamations, led by the school principal, Mr. Ekwa, as he invited the top 5 students from each class onto the stage, with Adiang among them, while the entire school erupted into applause. This spectacle triggered a competitive spirit, compelling each student to strive for excellence. It instilled a profound belief in being the best version of oneself, devoid of unnecessary comparison. The race, as they learned, wasn't against others; it was an inner journey to surpass one's previous self each day, with the ultimate aim of making the world a better place through sharing and aiding those in need. These were the cherished memories of the good old days.

Adiang's perspective on life had transformed significantly since his primary school days. Aspirations now evolved into intellectual understanding, and an insatiable thirst for knowledge consumed him.

Lycee Molyko: Where Dreams Take Flight

Mandela was released from prison in 1990, and the Pan African Institute, along with the radio station, organized a debate and speech day. All the colleges in the city were invited to the Town center. As the selected students took the stage to recite prepared poems or sing songs about Mandela, Adiang found himself unprepared, lacking a speech or a poem. However, having studied South African history from an encyclopedia sent by his sister in the USA, Adiang quickly jotted down notes on a piece of paper he borrowed from a classmate. He then approached the judges, requesting an opportunity to speak, even though he wasn't initially scheduled to address the audience. This marked the beginning of his dream to become somebody, echoing the words of Charles Dickens. Just as Adiang reached the final line of his impromptu speech and was about to step down from the stage, a journalist and jury member ascended the platform, lifted him up, and declared into the microphone, "What a great orator you are, son."

Each day, as he entered the school campus with the mindset of a winner, Lycee Molyko nurtured and reinforced that attitude in all aspects of student life. Lycee excelled in sports, consistently ranked among the top academically in the province, boasted some of the most beautiful girls in the city, and cultivated a culture of sartorial excellence among its male students. It was the province's sole bilingual school, an achievement unto itself. Lycee also housed remarkable music orchestras, stage play groups, and traditional dance ensembles, to name just a few.

The words of Muhammad Ali adorned the walls of Lycee, particularly in areas where students congregated. In the lead-up to the GCE exams, which were taken extremely seriously, motivational speakers were unheard of, yet the school had inscribed these lines by Muhammad Ali in various spots across the campus. The alumni of Lycee, now attending the University of Buea, often extended help to younger students.

Words of Wisdom and Inspiration

One person, in particular, stands out—an unforgettable social prefect and now a renowned journalist at FM 105 Douala—Mr. Behyia Leonard Bruce. Behyia, who was already emceeing events while in school, allowed Adiang to study within the university campus and even provided him with a place to sleep when he couldn't navigate the dark roads alone to go home. In Behyia, Adiang found inspiration for his aspiration to become a bilingual journalist. On the walls of Behyia's bedroom, the same words that adorned certain parts of the school building could be found like these:

> *"Don't count the days; make the days count."*
>
> *"It's not bragging if you can back it up."*

Burning Dreams of Greatness

Adiang's aspirations and dreams were fueled by what he witnessed daily on TV and heard on the radio. Voices like Peter Esoka, Eric Chinje, Zacharie Nkuo, Jean Lambert Nang, Fon Echekiye, Denise Epote, Joseph ChebonKeng Kalabubse, Dieudonné Pigui, and Enanga Kebbi, just to name a few, served as an inspiration to anyone aspiring to be a newscaster or work in radio and television. Adiang yearned for greatness, a desire to lift his mother out of the daily struggle.

The flame of greatness burned brightly in his heart, motivating him to excel in the BEPC (Brevet d'Études de

Premier Cycle) and GCE O-level exams, and ultimately propelling him to attend Lycee Classique in Limbe.

However, Adiang's defining moments occurred when he realized he couldn't easily afford what some of his friends had – new clothes, bicycles, sports attire with sneakers – while he made do with ordinary rubber shoes called "chan shoes" or "Batoula." He heard about parties that he was never part of, and he recognized that his family relied on him, unlike his friends who relied on their families. It was a crucial lesson: one day, his friends would move on, leaving him behind. The situation at home wouldn't change unless he remembered where he came from and the life his family lived.

> *"Son, never play the same game as them. They count on their families, but your family counts on you. Be very careful. Remember that one day these friends will all go away, and you'll be left alone. The situation at home will remain the same if you forget what family you come from, what type of life your family lives. There are those who succeed with the help of their parents, but you will have to succeed to help your family. You are not fighting the same fight. They were born on the right side of the shore, but you have to throw yourself into the river and face the crocodiles to succeed. Be very careful, son."*
>
> *- Nyanti*

Nyanti's words echoed in his head: "You are not fighting the same fight. They were born on the right side of the shore, but you have to throw yourself into the river and face the crocodiles to succeed." This realization led Adiang to walk his path alone, focusing on his studies and achieving remarkable results. Suddenly, everyone wanted to be his friend, and even the most beautiful girls paid him visits at his modest carabot house. But the seed of greatness had been firmly planted in him, and no distractions could sway his dreams and aspirations of becoming the person who could bring change to his household and family.

The Power of Ideas and Faith

Adiang found out that the lack of ideas on how to create wealth was his family's problem, not the lack of money. So, if they could get the ideas, his family could change the whole situation. But to get the idea, there was a need for constant studying, finding out, and then putting this information into a journal, because your head is not a memory card. The next best thing was repetition—going over it several times. Eventually, the idea takes roots and starts to grow, manifesting in your bank account, your wardrobe, your personality, and your lifestyle.

During these times, Christian faith upbringing influenced many families. Children were taught about heaven and hell, with the concept of facing damnation in hellfire if they were sinners. This concept worked well as a motivating factor. Uncle Mathias was in charge of disciplining those who failed exams, and Adiang swore he would never be subjected to Uncle Mathias's punishments. The only way to avoid that was by bringing home good results. Adiang couldn't bear the thought of spending eternity in hellfire, so he made a firm decision to avoid sinful behavior.

As a result, Adiang grew up ensuring he followed the rules of his parents and elders, praying to God and seeking forgiveness through confession at the Catholic Church whenever he committed a sin. Sunday church service attendance became a routine and a tradition in their household, with everyone present. The concept of hellfire, while perplexing, still earned Adiang's respect and kept him on the righteous path. The idea that old habits die hard resonated with many in their congregation.

Adiang and his friends looked at life strictly through biblical interpretations, but it often led to unanswered questions, with elders dismissing his inquiries as products of youthful curiosity.

Thanks to their adherence to Christianity, Adiang became a hardworking adult who understood that prayers alone were not enough without personal effort. The Bible states, "I will bless the work of your hands." It raised the question: What were you doing that you wanted God to bless? Were you merely praying and waiting for blessings, or were you actively pursuing your dreams? Adiang believed that God had already paved the way, and now it was his time to achieve his dreams.

Whatever you need in life is wrapped up in the word. When you get hold of it, keep saying it. Don't stop saying it.

The Bible says: 'In the city of Ephesus, so mightily grew the word of God and prevailed.'

"I have found the course that I must follow. In the name of Jesus, the Lord is my Shepherd; I shall not want. He makes me lie down in green pastures; He leads me beside the still waters. He restores my soul; He leads me in the paths of righteousness for His name's sake. Even though I walk through the valley of the shadow of death, I will fear no evil; for You are with me; Your rod and Your staff, they comfort me. You prepare a table before me in the presence of my enemies; You anoint my head with oil; my cup runs over. Surely goodness and mercy shall follow me all the days of my life, and I will dwell in the house of the Lord forever. Amen...."

You must be ready to pay the price for what you want in life. There's no such thing as getting what you want without paying the price. If what you want means so much to you, you must be willing to pay the price for it. Some people want it so badly that they are ready to pay any price, while others step back because they find the price too high for their desires. This truth applies to every step we take in our lives.

In these powerful words, Adiang found guidance, inspiration, and a sense of purpose to drive him toward his dreams and aspirations.

> "The smallest seeds of today's negligence will bloom into tomorrow's biggest regrets. One day, your life will flash before your eyes. Make sure it's worth watching. Have a purpose in life, and let it be the reason you wake up every morning. Do what you love, do what you're good at, do what the world needs, and do what you can be paid for."
>
> *– Nyanti*

3

The Music Event

The Limbe Community field was teeming with people of all ages, eagerly gathered to witness the music event sponsored by Delta Cigarettes. The main attraction of the evening was none other than the renowned artist, Lapiro de Mbanga, often referred to as "Ndinga Man," the Man of the People. Lapiro's songs resonated deeply with the masses, and he was adored all across the country at this stage of his career, with his hit song "Mimba We" translating to "Remember Us" in English.

The field was packed to capacity, as everyone was eager to see Lapiro's electrifying performance. Adiang and his friends wasted no time, leaving the school compound and rushing home to change into their finest attire before making their way to the community field. They were determined not to miss a single moment of this musical extravaganza. As the kids settled on the grass near the stage, the adults stood behind them, indulging in cigarettes and beer, both of which were being promoted at a discounted price as part of the event.

The show began with various artists warming up the stage for Lapiro. The atmosphere was electric, and the crowd couldn't

Digging For Life: The Music Event

contain their excitement. When Lapiro and his crew finally graced the stage, guided by a contingent of police officers, the energy was palpable. The massive stage, constructed mostly from iron and wooden planks, provided the perfect platform for Lapiro to work his magic.

As Lapiro launched into his first song, the crowd erupted with ecstatic dancing, clapping, and expressions of sheer joy. Suddenly, Lapiro interrupted the music and called for his dancers to take a break. In a surprising move, he invited two children—a boy and a girl—to join him on stage. Adiang, renowned in his school and neighborhood as the best dancer, wasted no time leaping to his feet, eager to climb onto the stage.

However, his moment of glory was nearly snatched away as a man, perhaps a relative, forcefully pushed him back and thrust forward another child. Undeterred, Lapiro, upon noticing the injustice, halted the proceedings and pointed directly at Adiang. He insisted that Adiang ascend the stage with another young girl he had chosen.

With unwavering determination, Adiang mounted the stage and danced alongside Lapiro. The audience was captivated, and Adiang's electrifying performance was a sight to behold. This pivotal moment not only earned him the title of the best dancer but also garnered him a trophy and a dozen boxes of Delta-branded polo shirts.

After the show, Adiang became the star of the day, with a crowd surrounding him to offer their congratulations.

A photographer handed him a Kodak color photo of his unforgettable dance performance with Lapiro. Accompanied by an entourage from the Community field, Adiang returned home.

Nyanti, initially fearing that Adiang had caused trouble, was pleasantly surprised when the crowd began singing his praises. They explained what an incredible son she had, and Nyanti's heart swelled with pride as Adiang presented her with his trophy, the cherished photo, and a stack of polo shirts.

Nyanti's beaming smile as she placed the Kodak picture on the living room wall expressed the deep affection she felt for her son. This photograph would later find its place in the family album, but it always held a prominent position on the wall, a testament to the moment that had changed their lives forever.

Adiang swiftly became the new sensation in Limbe, invited to showcase his dancing prowess at various events, including birthday parties and special occasions. His electrifying performances garnered admiration and adoration from all quarters. Everywhere he went, Adiang was celebrated, and friendships flourished as he etched his name as the finest Makossa dancer in town.

This pivotal moment sparked a newfound passion in Adiang—performing arts. He began to envision himself as a performer, not just a dancer. Adiang stepped out of his comfort zone, venturing into uncharted territories where he sang and danced, pushing the boundaries of his imagination. In due course, he joined his college orchestra, further nurturing his artistic talents.

This transformative event paved the way for Adiang's extraordinary journey as an international television star, but the destination was far from the remote corner of Africa where he began. Brazil, of all places, became the stage for his meteoric rise, where he shone brightly in television commercials, series, and telenovelas, fluently switching between Portuguese and Spanish.

As a reader, you might wonder how Adiang found himself in Brazil, a land with languages foreign to his upbringing. That, my friends, is a tale for another day—an adventure filled with twists and turns that defied all odds.

But always remember, Adiang made a solemn vow and a life-changing decision, one that reverberates within us all:

You must be ready to pay the price of what you want in life; there's no such thing as achieving your desires without paying the price. If what you want holds great value to you, you must be willing to pay the price to attain it.

Adiang's unwavering commitment was fueled by a profound desire to provide Nyanti with a better life. This exemplifies the extraordinary power of decision-making that children and young people possess—a power capable of altering the course of their lives and shaping their destinies.

The Call To South Africa

The Iddle Park, a place where they had spent countless hours in their youth, reminiscing about life's possibilities while indulging in the vices of the moment—smoking weed, sipping on beer, and discussing the triumphs of others. It was in this very park that destiny summoned them once more.

On this particular Friday morning, the rain descended with unrelenting fervor. Adiang and everyone present held onto hope, praying for respite by evening, for Fridays were sacred—reserved for the nocturnal revelry of clubbing. Amidst the musings, a sudden collision near Larry's barbershop disrupted our discourse. Excitement coursed through their veins as they rushed to embrace the newcomer, shouting his name in euphoria. He was no ordinary visitor; he was a "Bushfaller"—one who had ventured abroad and returned, bearing the fruits of triumph and prosperity.

Chimolo Pem, once a familiar face, had transformed. He stood before them, larger than life, immaculately attired, and exuding the fragrance of success. His tales of life abroad unfolded like scripture, captivating all like devout disciples, hanging on every word of a man recounting heavenly experiences, even though he himself had never set foot in paradise. The collective yearning to ascend to that celestial realm—to follow in Chimolo Pem's footsteps—was palpable. But the audacity to embark on the uncharted path, especially by road, remained elusive.

In those days, the journey to foreign lands was a pursuit reserved for the affluent and the audacious. Dreaming of the unattainable was futile; it could only be admired from afar. Thus, their role became one of admiration, celebrating Chimolo Pem's achievements and listening with rapt attention to the sagas of those who had ventured to Europe.

However, as Chimolo regaled us with the allure of life abroad, he saved the most astonishing revelation for last. After recounting the splendor and opportunities that awaited beyond our borders, Pakatolo Aghen, known as the Town Commissioner in our frequented Iddle Park, interjected with a probing question:

Pakatolo: "If that place is so good, why did you come back?"

Tima Baron, the local barber, interjected, attempting to deter Aghen from disrupting our cherished moments of illusory joy. They craved these stories, whether true or fabricated, as long as the beer flowed and the tales enthralled us.

Larry: "He's on vacation, bro. Please, stop interrupting."

Aghen: "As the commissioner, I have the right to know the truth, so we don't lead our friends into the unknown. Who knows, this guy might have been repatriated, carrying an illness that could infect us all."

This time, Tchakuna, the phone booth operator, stormed into the salon and effectively quashed Aghen's civil interruption. The news that Chimolo Pem had returned to town had spread like wildfire.

Tchakuna: "Old boy, leave these low-life folks. Let's head upstairs to the phone booth and discuss real matters."

Chimolo found himself pulled in every direction, some urging him to stay, others seeking to lead him away to a quieter spot where they could savor the contents of his wallet without the clamor of the crowd. Amid the confusion, Bobbychaps, another Iddle Park regular, raised his voice:

Bobby Chaps: "Chimolo, where did you come from? We never threw you a send-off party. We last heard you were in Libya, and suddenly, you're back. What's going on?"

Chimolo Pem's response on that day left many disheartened. He revealed that he had been caught attempting to enter Spain and was subsequently repatriated. Pakatolo couldn't contain his glee:

Pakatolo: "I knew it! I knew it! I'm the commissioner in this town; I verify every piece of information. I knew it!"

Bobby Chaps: "Shut your mouth! Just because we call you commissioner doesn't make you a real one. Besides, we ought to encourage the guy. At least he attempted something most of us here wouldn't dare. Most of you rely on your families to send you abroad, but he went alone, with little money. You've got to commend him for that."

Tchakuna: "What?! That's impossible! I can't imagine seeing Europe and then being repatriated and agreeing to come back. How can you enter paradise and willingly return to hell? No way, it's not true! Old boy, please tell us what happened..." (The irony was that years later, rumors circulated that Tchakuna had been repatriated at Brussels Airport. Lesson: Never say never...)

Chimolo: "Guys, it's true. You all know we're like brothers here, and I gain nothing from lying to you. But I am going back."

This declaration stunned some, with laughter from a few and disbelief from others.

Chimolo: "Who wants to come with me?"

Pakalolo, chiming in: "I'm telling you all now, this guy is crazy. You know these white folks inject all sorts of things into people before sending them back. Chimolo is nuts, and his family should take him to the hospital."

Chimolo Pem then embarked on an eloquent narrative of his entire journey, from its inception to its abrupt conclusion. He extended an invitation to anyone who possessed the courage to join him on this new journey, for he had meticulously planned each step. This time, there would be no turning back; he was determined to reach his destination and change the course of his life and that of his family.

Adiang grew increasingly close to Chimolo Pem, extracting invaluable information about travel requirements and the stages of the journey to the fabled destination. One evening, while enjoying drinks at the famed Sea Palace snack bar on Church Street, Adiang confided in Chimolo about his intention to travel. He implored Chimolo to speak with his family, as they had lost faith in him due to his dropout status and perceived lack of direction. Chimolo, proving to be a true friend, agreed to assist Adiang, offering counsel on the courage and wisdom necessary for the journey.

> Chimolo: "Be the last to speak in any gathering. Don't reveal your weaknesses or ignorance. Even if you know the answer, remain silent and only speak when prompted. This way, you'll navigate through uncharted territory."

A Mother's Dilemma

Nyanti had just returned from church on a Sunday morning, still in the spiritual mood of the gospel, and was engaged in her household chores when the two adventurous young men arrived at her doorstep. They greeted her in the local Pidgin English.

"Reme how far? (Mom, how are you doing?)" they asked.

Nyanti motioned for them to come into the living room and, inquired in their dialect about the identity of the young man accompanying her son and the purpose of their visit. Chimolo began an unexpected but captivating narrative about his family, highlighting that his mom was also a member of the Saint Jude prayer group, just like Nyanti. He shared how his mother had encouraged him to embark on this journey. Chimolo went on to recount the story of Nelson Mandela and how he had transformed South Africa into a new Eldorado for all black people worldwide—a land of opportunities with free education, housing, and monthly allowances. He skillfully weaved in elements of the Church, education, and a brighter future to persuade Nyanti. Intrigued, she immediately inquired about the financial requirements for the journey.

Meanwhile, Ajietoh de Paris, Adiang's older brother, had just arrived and overheard the discussion. He promptly intervened, attempting to dissuade Nyanti from investing in this venture.

> Ajietoh: (In Pidgin English) "Nyanti, what are you thinking? These people are not to be trusted. They'll take your money and spend it on drinks at DMX (a bar in Mile One)."

He continued, "You want to give them all this money? I've already completed my education, and no one gave me money to go to Ivory Coast for further studies. Now you want to give money to these drinkers?"

Nyanti was no stranger to Ajietoh's emotional appeals and understood her children well. In the midst of this, Adiang remained silent.

Jean Claude, another of Nyanti's sons, interjected:

> Jean Claude: "Leave that aside. This man will succeed; I can see it in his eyes. He really wants to go, and

his spirit is no longer here; he is ready to embark on this journey."

As Nyanti weighed her options, a mother's dilemma unfolded.

The Journey Begins

Everything fell into place just as planned. On a Sunday, after church, when God was still fresh in Nyanti's mind, and on a Monday morning, Jean Claude, Chimolo, and Adiang found themselves on a bus headed to Buea to obtain a crucial travel document—a passport for Adiang. Jean Claude expedited the passport application, and it was ready for pickup later that same day.

The small vans that Adiang took to leave Cameroon. These Saviem (French) vans transport passengers to the border city of Sakambo, where you must cross the Congo River into Ouessou, the first city of the Republic of Congo (Brazzaville).

The small vans that Adiang took to leave Cameroon. These Saviem (French) vans transport passengers to the border city of Sakambo, where you must cross the Congo River into Ouessou, the first city of the Republic of Congo (Brazzaville).

Two days later, Adiang stood before Nyanti, bidding her goodbye. She blessed him with a heartfelt prayer, handed him some money, and gave him a white rosary, reminding him never to forsake his faith. Adiang nodded in agreement.

Chimolo had imparted valuable advice to Adiang: keep their plans confidential. He also provided the rendezvous point at the bus station where they would meet before embarking on their journey. Adiang, in turn, enlisted the help of his trusted and capable best friend and cousin, Nzie. Together, they joined Chimolo at the Mile 4 bus stop, where they would catch a bus to Douala, the economic capital.

As they sat in the bus, Nyanti's words continued to resonate in Adiang's mind, while Chimolo regaled him with tales of the success awaiting them in the diaspora. The journey had begun.

> *"Son, never play the same game as them. They count on their families, but your family counts on you. Be very careful. Remember that one day these friends will all go away, and you'll be left alone. The situation at home will remain the same if you forget what family you come from, what type of life your family lives. There are those who succeed with the help of their parents, but you will have to succeed to help your family. You are not fighting the same fight. They were born on the right side of the shore, but you have to throw yourself into the river and face the crocodiles to succeed. Be very careful, son."*
>
> *- Nyanti*

Adiang had seen and heard about many friends who went abroad, returned, and transformed their families' lives. Boys and girls who, like him, were dropouts but came back with substantial wealth, building mansions for their parents and owning luxury cars. Some were patiently waiting for their turn to travel, knowing that their relatives already abroad would finance their visas and expenses to Europe. Adiang, however, had no such support and had no choice but to take the challenging path—the only path.

He remembered a movie he watched as a child about an American soldier with little guerilla warfare experience who had to survive in the Vietnamese forest during the war. Adiang's journey was like that—on foot and with little to no money. The story of Mandela, who spent 27 years in prison only to become the President of a powerful nation, served as a powerful motivation for him. It was clear that all things are possible for those who believe. Endurance had become meaningless; Adiang had mentally endured whatever challenges lay ahead on this journey.

He pondered the irony that many of the great figures of their time had faced immense hardships to become world references. So why fear embracing the unknown? He encouraged himself and others to keep trying and striving, for success lay ahead in the place of excellence.

Adiang had high hopes of arriving safely in South Africa, the first step in his journey to return to school. Education was the key, as his teachers had always emphasized. They even had a daily song about it before entering the classrooms.

As they traveled to Douala, he and Chimolo were undecided about which city in South Africa to settle in. Cape Town, Pretoria, and Johannesburg were incredibly beautiful cities, rivaling those in Europe. Adiang aspired to secure a high-profile job after completing his education, traveling the world as a journalist and reporter to share stories of people, places, and events with those who couldn't travel. These stories would reach people in their living rooms through their TV screens.

Adiang knew that his only chance was to obtain a high-paying job after his education to support Nyanti before her time came. He made a solemn promise in that bus to Douala that Nyanti would one day fly in a plane and visit foreign lands, just like the other mothers in Mile 1, before her time came.

The dream would be fulfilled later in life...

> Love is all about becoming the right person, not about finding the right person. Become the kind of person you want to spend the rest of your life with, and those who deserve you will naturally gravitate toward you. The actions you take to become the person you aspire to be are what differentiate your current self from your desired self.
>
> – *Nyanti*

4

An Encounter with Mike Tyson

The Sea Palace buzzed with the excited chatter of boxing fans. It was January 16th, 1999, and the MGM Grand Garden Arena was hosting a much-anticipated fight – a special night for sports enthusiasts in Limbe. Hours before the bout, fans gathered eagerly in front of the big screen to witness their hero, Mike Tyson, in action. This match was particularly controversial, pitting Iron Mike, an African American, against Francois Botha, a white South African. The controversy stemmed from the historical context of Apartheid in South Africa, which was still fresh in the memories of many Cameroonian spectators.

Due to the time difference between Cameroon and the United States, the fight was set to begin at almost 3 am local time. Nevertheless, Sea Palace was packed to the brim with boxing enthusiasts. Adiang and his friends had arrived early to secure seats in front of the bartender while sipping on a shared bottle of Coca-Cola. However, as the night wore on, most of his friends had succumbed to sleep, and two had decided to head home, mindful of the impending school day.

As the fight got underway, the vibrant streets of Church Street began to take on their nocturnal hues. The night girls, known as Ashawos, began to populate the streets, soliciting potential customers for their services. Sea Palace was renowned for attracting high-profile clients, and it wasn't long before Adiang and his friend were politely asked to vacate their seats.

They were asked to leave the bar because they were young, didn't spend on alcoholic drinks, and didn't interact with the night ladies present. These girls were strategic partners of the bar, as they enticed men to come in, spend generously on alcohol, and later accompany them home or to nearby establishments.

By the time the Tyson vs. Botha showdown commenced, Adiang and his remaining friend found themselves clinging to the grated walls and tables for a mere glimpse of the action. The hall was filled to capacity, resonating with the fervent cheers and shouts of support, some driven by bets and others by the sheer desire to see a black man, a brother in their eyes, emerge victorious.

Adiang, an ardent fan of Iron Mike, observed from his corner on a large table slightly above most of the adults in front of him. Though it was a bit challenging, he managed to catch glimpses of the pivotal moments of the fight. He began to notice that Botha had the upper hand in the beginning, landing jabs on Tyson. It seemed to him that Tyson was hunting for a knockout punch. This suspicion was confirmed in the 5th round when Tyson connected with a short right hand that sent Botha tumbling to the canvas. Botha struggled to rise but stumbled back into the ropes before finally collapsing to the mat, unable to beat the referee Richard Steele's 10-count.

By this late hour of the night, the usually tranquil city was jolted awake by the raucous celebration at the Sea Palace. It felt as though the Indomitable Lions had defeated Argentina with Diego Maradona at the opening of the 1990 World Cup in Italy. The crowd erupted in joy, tables and chairs were kicked about, voices were raised in jubilation, and some even spoke in tongues. Tears of joy flowed, and a few stood in a trance, their eyes glued to the TV in disbelief. A handful rushed out to neighboring bars to share the good news, while a small number who had bet against Tyson found solace in his victory, separating business from emotional support or fanaticism.

For the entire week that followed, newspapers, TV, radios, and conversations were dominated by the name Mike Tyson. He had become the hero of his era, often compared to the legendary Muhammad Ali.

Weeks later, life returned to its usual rhythm, but Adiang continued to rehearse the commentary of the match for his friends. During school breaks, they would gather around him, eager to hear his vivid retelling of the fight. Adiang took pleasure in recounting the match, occasionally adding fictitious elements to enhance his storytelling skills. Little did he know that one day, his connection with Mike Tyson would become a reality.

Lights, Camera, Dreams

New York City appeared even more enchanting to Adiang than he had ever imagined. It was a surreal experience to find himself strolling through the bustling streets of this great metropolis—a place where any child from his hometown would give anything for the chance to visit, regardless of the cost. Times Square, in all its luminous glory, dazzled him, and he couldn't help but marvel at the sheer magnitude of the lights. It was a stark contrast to the majority of his childhood, which he had spent studying by the dim glow of kerosene lamps.

Each day, Adiang embarked on a train journey from Harlem to Downtown Manhattan's Broadway district. Here, he was immersing himself in the world of stage plays and on-camera skills for actors at the prestigious TVI Actors Studio, nestled in the heart of Times Square. After making a name for himself in Brazilian TV, stage plays, TV commercials, and movies, Adiang yearned to test the waters of Hollywood. Aware that the path to success could be unexpectedly arduous, he was determined to prepare himself meticulously, even if it meant a prolonged journey. The refrain of his primary school song, "Education is the key," echoed in his mind, reminding him to do things the right way so that when opportunity knocked, he'd be well-prepared.

The golden opportunity he had longed for arrived in the form of a fully paid four-month hybrid course—a chance to learn the intricacies of Hollywood-style acting. Adiang enrolled in this specialized training at the TVI Actors Studio, guided by Hollywood professionals: On-Camera Skills by Magaly Collimon & Justin MacCarthy, Voice and Diction by Patricia Mauceri, Alexander Technique by Patrick Mellen, and Improvisation by Joe Osheroff.

The TVI Actors Studio didn't just provide instruction; it offered students weekly casting opportunities with some of the best managers, casting directors, and producers from Hollywood. These auditions were direct gateways to coveted roles in Hollywood films, anywhere in the world. It's essential to grasp that these classes catered to professionals already in the acting and filmmaking industry. The sheer number of hours students dedicated to rehearsing monologues and scenes was astounding.

The support and commitment of the teachers were unwavering, perhaps because the tuition fees were substantial. As some teachers reiterated in class, "You've paid a premium to be here, and you deserve the best. If you encounter any difficulties or need assistance with your lines, don't hesitate to reach out." This encouragement spurred Adiang to work harder than ever before, resulting in numerous paid roles in short films and stage plays. While feature films and blockbusters required a work permit he didn't possess at the time, Adiang's goal had been to acquire the skills necessary to secure international roles in Brazil, and he succeeded admirably.

This journey underscores a fundamental truth: To achieve your goals and dreams in life, meticulous planning and adherence to the rules are paramount. Keep working diligently, and one day, you may find yourself at the pinnacle of your field, a source of inspiration to many.

TVI was a school that upheld rigorous standards, with zero tolerance for tardiness. They prepared students not just to land Hollywood acting jobs but also to retain them, emphasizing the importance of humility both on set and during auditions. The mantra was clear: Rehearse your lines thoroughly before stepping into any audition, immerse yourself in the character, and avoid unnecessary questions—just be yourself.

Adiang was spending the remaining weeks of his vacation from school in Maryland, a city often likened to "Cameroon in miniature" in the United States. As he prepared for his return to Brazil, he received an email from his Brazilian agent, hinting at a potentially significant job in Sao Paulo alongside an American superstar, though the name remained undisclosed. Adiang recognized that opportunities like this were rare and promptly dialed his agent's number in Brazil. She inquired whether he could be in Brazil that weekend for an audition, providing limited details about the job.

Booking a direct flight, Adiang arrived at the audition venue in Vila Madalena, São Paulo, on a Saturday morning. The hall was teeming with actors auditioning and extras experimenting with props. Upon spotting him from a distance, his agent exclaimed in Portuguese, "Voce veio!" which translates to "You came!"

Dressed akin to Will.i.am of the Black Eyed Peas, Adiang navigated the bustling crowd toward his agent, and they warmly embraced. The audition proceeded seamlessly, and upon leaving the set, the director approached Adiang and congratulated him on securing the role. His agent praised how his attire and charisma had played perfectly into the character they were seeking—someone with his unique charisma and naturally radiant smile. It became evident that his investment in the Actors Studio had not been a waste of time or money. As they say, invest in yourself.

Up until the day of filming, none of the casting crew were aware that Mike Tyson was the superstar of this million-dollar commercial for Brazilian SKOL beer. All preparations had been made, and the actors had been rehearsing tirelessly since morning. Filming commenced around 2 pm, and at 3 pm, Iron Mike made his grand entrance, arriving with three bodyguards and his manager. The director wasted no time, promptly shouting, "Action!" to commence filming his scenes.

Adiang meeting Mike Tyson

During a short break, Adiang, still incredulous that he was sharing the same filming set with the legendary world boxing champion Mike Tyson, seized the opportunity to strike up a conversation with Mike's bodyguards. Adiang contemplated the reason why all phones had been collected before entering the set—to prevent any unauthorized photographs with the champ. With trembling anticipation, Adiang approached and greeted the living legend, fully aware that this space was reserved for the lead roles, of which he was now a part.

Dreams Beyond Limitations

Just a reminder to the youths of today: In the 80s and 90s, being an African on the continent meant that one could only dream of seeing Tyson on TV screens, in magazines, or newspapers, never standing beside him. If you dared to express such a dream to a friend or relative, they would look at you as if you were nuts and advise you to stop dreaming. It seemed almost impossible to harbor such a dream. However, I implore you to dream, folks—dream higher and beyond every limitation. Remember that dreams are just dreams; the key is to chase after them.

To some, dreams require no effort, as the stars belong to the sky, just as we belong to this planet. Our paths may intersect or diverge as nature dictates, or perhaps it's all part of God's plan.

In this incredible moment, Tyson, the amazingly friendly superstar, shakes hands with Adiang and inquires about his place of origin. After securing Tyson's permission, Adiang swiftly retrieves his iPhone, capturing the moment with a photo, thanks to the assistance of one of Tyson's bodyguards. This single snapshot sends the Brazilian social media into a frenzy.

At that precise moment, Adiang reflects on his childhood in Limbe and the night of the fight at Sea Palace when Tyson defeated Botha. It's astonishing how his imagination and childhood dreams have led him to this surreal moment, a dream come true in an unexpected and unique way. No one could dismiss it as anything other than real, as he sits among fellow cast members on a film set, deconstructing his role.

Years later, the photograph and video clip from the commercial open numerous doors in both the entertainment industry and various aspects of life for Adiang. Within the African community in Brazil, he is regarded as a reference and star who rightfully represents Africa and Cameroon in the diaspora. Stardom takes one to another level of life, where favors come from every direction, and everyone wants a picture with you when you're around. You become a household name, and your friends even win over romantic partners by showing them your picture, claiming you as their brother or childhood friend. It's a phenomenon that Adiang finds amusing, as he doesn't quite comprehend how it works, but it exemplifies the saying: "Show me who your friends are, and I'll tell you who you are." If you aspire to success, walk with successful people; if you aim to become an engineer, associate with engineers, and so on.

> "What people think about you is none of your business; it changes with circumstances. Stop trying to seek love from others; instead, love yourself above all else. Don't seek recognition from others; instead, be true to yourself."
>
> – *Nyanti*

5

Christian Upbringing

In the heart of many impoverished families in Cameroon, a glimmer of hope often leads them to embrace religion, seeking a miraculous transformation or an escape from their persistent poverty. They become devout churchgoers, even if their lives don't necessarily align with the teachings of the gospel, in the expectation that a miracle will suddenly elevate them from poverty to prosperity.

In these families, the father typically serves as the sole breadwinner, while the mother assumes the role of a full-time homemaker. She devotes herself entirely to her husband and children, ensuring their needs are met in exchange for their individual quests. Every market day, usually on Fridays, the father entrusts the weekly budget to his wife, who then manages the household to the best of her abilities with the limited resources at hand.

This budget would have been sufficient if it only had to support mom, dad, and their kids. To truly appreciate how mothers navigate their limited budgets, one would need to follow someone like Nyanti to Limbe's main market and experience firsthand the intricate dance of family management. Over time spent in English Cameroon, Nyanti had honed the skills necessary for her family's survival and her own.

When she first arrived in Limbe, she couldn't speak a word of Pidgin English. However, today, she confidently negotiates prices for merchandise and even has her own spot in the market. Limbe's market is divided into sections, each catering to specific types of goods. The meat section is conveniently located near the slaughterhouse, ensuring that customers can easily purchase their meat. Likewise, the sections for garri and peanuts are nearby, while the vegetable market occupies the northern part of the market.

On the other hand, the clothing section is situated close to the restaurants, as it serves as a place for relaxation. Here, you can leisurely browse through the best dresses, shoes, hats, suits, and more, all while enjoying a plate of water fufu and eru, rice and beans, fufucorn and vegetables, or even a serving of cornchaff with a bottle of cold 33 Export or Guinness beer by your side as you choose your attire.

Although Nyanti came from a family of traditional healers, she embraced Christianity with fervor, even while maintaining her connections to her childhood and influential traditional spiritual practices, which many considered to be juju or witchcraft. She firmly believed that God is good all the time and saw the forest as a gift for sustenance and healing when illness struck. Despite her knowledge of spiritual incantations, she refrained from using them after becoming a member of the Saint Jude prayer group at the Catholic church in New Town.

Interestingly, Nyanti was never allowed to share her dreams, as her husband couldn't forgive her for foreseeing his mother's death in a dream two weeks before it happened in real life. Occasionally, during moonlit nights, Nyanti would gather her children and recount the harrowing stories of the Maquisard war that forced her and her husband to flee to English Cameroon. In these rare moments, she would share tales from her village, some mythical and others rooted in reality. She narrated them so vividly that they felt as real as only she could make them. Among these stories were the mysteries surrounding the twin lakes of Mouanenguba, particularly the male lake, which no one could enter without the chief's permission and hope to emerge alive.

Adiang returned home early from school due to a fever. Nyanti, his mother, used a damp cloth to help lower her son's body temperature. She left him resting on the sofa while she prepared dinner for the family. Adiang woke up suddenly, feeling a cold sensation on his thighs. Out of nowhere, a viper had coiled itself around the boy's legs. Nyanti entered the room and instructed her son not to move or harm the snake. She carefully picked up the snake and placed it by the door. As the snake slithered away, she jokingly told her son, "That's your brother, who came to check on you and see how you are doing. You wouldn't want to harm your brother, would you?"

Startled, Adiang nodded in agreement, having no intention of harming his newfound "brother."

On another occasion, Adiang and his brother, Njike, faced occasional mistreatment from a young lady who believed that their frequent visits to eat her mother's Achu food without contributing were excessive ("Langa-throat," as it's known in Pidgin English for glutton). Despite the fact that her mother willingly offered them food, this lady couldn't tolerate them eating for free. Fueled by her unkindness, the two boys decided to invoke the power of African spirituality. There's an African adage that says, "Never awaken a sleeping cobra."

In response to the girl's unjust actions, Adiang and Njike joined their hands together and chanted some unfamiliar incantations. They then uttered the words in Pidgin English, "Ya belle go bite," meaning "you'll have stomach ache."

Two days later, late at night, there were thunderous knocks at the front door. Everyone in the household awoke to find the girl and her parents standing there, seeking forgiveness for their daughter. She had been suffering from severe bellyaches for two days. After about 45 minutes of discussion and negotiation, Nyanti approached her sons. With a simple gesture, they put their hands together and uttered a few words, instantly relieving the girl of her pain. That night marked the end of the girl's interactions with the boys, the boys later learned that her parents had sent her to live with her aunt in Bamenda, the capital city of the North West province.

In an effort to break the cycle of retaliation, Nyanti and her husband initiated morning and evening prayer sessions in their home, along with obligatory church services every Sunday for all members of their household. They had also taken the boys for a cleansing session with the ancestral spirits in their village. Morning prayer sessions, led by Nyanti's husband, began with the Lord's Prayer, followed by the "Hail Mary." The Stations of the Cross followed, which was the longest part. Adiang often felt like quitting, especially as his father recited the prayers slowly and loudly, as if to ensure the words penetrated the family's souls. Eventually, the children memorized every word, and the prayers became an integral part of their daily lives. As scripture best puts it, "Teach a child the way they should go, and when they are old, they will not depart from it."

The fear of God is the beginning of wisdom: was the password to make her kids understand that without God, nothing is possible, and with God, all things are possible for those who believe in Him. Who doesn't want to change their lifestyle from poverty to richness by just believing in God and receiving the miraculous life-changing effects? But that was the wrong equation, which Nyanti quickly saw and decided to make a change, for it doesn't suffice to only believe but to work hard to achieve your dreams. So if she can't work like her husband, then she must create a job for herself, as she said repeatedly, "Help yourself, and the Heavens shall help you." Prayer is not sufficient if you do nothing, as God can only bless the work of your hands.

Nyanti became an entrepreneur overnight and without any prior experience. She had been keeping some cash whenever her husband gave her the weekly money for foodstuffs for the family. SONARA was being constructed, and Nyanti was one of the first women to obtain certification to supply food to the laborers every day. Her household became her partners as the kids took turns in her kitchen to help her cook the different meals each day. As early as 4 am, everyone was up and doing something. She would wake everyone with these words: "No food for the lazy man."

Eventually, her kids, as they were growing, mastered the art of cooking various meals, which made her so proud. The feeling of accomplishment came when she financially helped her husband buy a small farmland at mile 1 near the General hospital to grow the crops that she now sells at the small bigmouth market for some extra money to manage her household.

Nyanti believed in prayers and hard work. She was exemplary in her very few words and great actions that contributed hugely to the positive changes and developments in her family. Nyanti had successfully instilled in each of her kids the values and essence of living a better life. Only faith, hard work, and faith again in God and in your dreams can make you achieve your craziest dreams, which to many is impossible. She says, "Challenge the impossible always, go for it, and be the winner that you were made to be." Her legacy shall live forever as she invested in them the spirit of no fear and to dare into the unknown, knowing that there is a goal that must be achieved no matter the cost. Do what is in your reach, and leave what's not for God to do. Most of all, be quiet about it, don't be overly anxious or worried, just be calm, as it shall come to pass at the right time. God's time is the best.

Nyanti's Guide to Life:

"Be your own hero. Improve focus, guard your privacy, endure challenges, and act strategically. Embrace authenticity, cultivate persistence, and let actions speak louder than words. Focus on self-improvement, take calculated risks, and maintain discipline. Choose your companions wisely, build self-esteem, and believe in yourself. Success is an ongoing journey."

It's remarkable how Nyanti consistently and repeatedly utters these words whenever she encourages her children to strive for excellence in any endeavor, whether it's related to their studies or household chores. It's quite astonishing to think that she never had the opportunity to attend school or receive a formal education. One can only attribute her wisdom to divine inspiration or her tenacious and rich life experiences.

> Get up and be your own hero. Don't blame the distraction; improve your focus. Don't share too much; privacy is power. Hard times never last, but enduring people do. Move in silence; speak only when it is time to say checkmate. Be authentic; live with integrity. Don't wait for opportunities to present themselves; create them. Persistence is the key to success. Let your actions speak louder than your words. Don't compare yourself to others; just be better than the person you were yesterday. Take calculated risks and learn from your failures. Discipline is the foundation of success. Choose your companions carefully. Surround yourself with people who lift you up. Cultivate self-esteem and believe in your abilities. Success is not a goal but a constant journey of personal improvement.

– Nyanti

Part 2

TRIALS AND TRIBULATIONS

"Work hard to become the best version of yourself—for yourself. Don't pretend to be something you're not. Believe in yourself, question everything, and surround yourself with people who uplift you rather than tear you down. You've got one life, and this is it. Strive to be the best version of yourself."

– Nyanti

6

A Quest for Greatness

"Never forget where you come from, but always know where you are going. It's not for you to figure out 'why,' but to figure out 'how' to achieve greatness. It's not your fault to come from a humble family, but it becomes your responsibility if you do nothing to improve your situation."

These were the words of wisdom Nyanti imparted to Adiang throughout his childhood. Coming from a humble family, Adiang understood the weight of poverty all too well. Early morning prayer sessions and a workload unfit for a child, Christmases with hand-me-downs or no new clothes at all, and long treks to school from mile 1 to Downbeach, sometimes barefoot because he couldn't afford sandals—these were the harsh realities of his upbringing.

To make ends meet, Adiang scavenged Limbe Botanical Garden for mangoes and other fruits since he had no money to buy food at the school cafeteria. He even resorted to eating rotten coconuts found by the sea, resulting in embarrassing and smelly consequences in class. Sometimes, he had to rely on the kindness of friends for a bite of puff puff, beans, fish roll, or meat pie during breaks. It was during these moments that Adiang became an expert in deciphering who would share their food and who wouldn't.

While the wealth of others didn't particularly bother him, the unanswered questions about his own poverty and struggles haunted him. Why did he have to endure such hardships while many of his friends had everything they needed? Nyanti's words echoed in his mind like the morning church bells announcing the first mass of the day.

Adiang couldn't help but ponder these rhetorical questions as he immersed himself in his studies, realizing that education was the path to a brighter future, as he was frequently reminded. At this point, if someone had told him that talent and creativity could shape his life's journey, he might not have believed it. Nevertheless, Adiang had secretly sworn to himself that he would not only elevate his own lifestyle to one of abundance but also make his parents proud by providing them with a better life, just like any child from a humble background dreams of.

"Son, never play the same game as them. They count on their families, but your family counts on you. Be very careful. Remember that one day these friends will all go away, and you'll be left alone. The situation at home will remain the same if you forget what family you come from, what type of life your family lives. There are those who succeed with the help of their parents, but you will

have to succeed to help your family. You are not fighting the same fight. They were born on the right side of the shore, but you have to throw yourself into the river and face the crocodiles to succeed. Be very careful, son."

- Nyanti

A Vision Beyond Childhood Labor

From a very young age, Adiang found himself in the role of a fisherman, working alongside the Awasha fishermen at Downbeach. He assisted them in launching their massive wooden canoes into the ocean, helped retrieve the fish from the nets, and later aided Nyanti in drying or smoking the fish over a wooden fireside, using what the locals called "mbanda," an Indian bamboo grill suspended just above the flames where Nyanti cooked daily. While his friends enjoyed playing football, a sport he was passionate about like any Cameroonian child, Adiang had to sell bananas, peanuts, or fried canda (locally made fried cow skin with tomatoes) by carrying a tray on his head and traversing the city from morning until late in the evening, often returning home utterly exhausted.

Adiang made a conscious decision to attend college outside of Limbe, primarily to escape the shame of child labor. Some may argue that child labor is noble, but at that time, it was a source of embarrassment, with his classmates often mocking him at the slightest opportunity. What saved him from relentless teasing was his academic prowess; he consistently ranked among the top three students during exams. Anyone who mocked Adiang knew that he would not assist them with class exercises, homework, or, needless to say, exams.

Without a predefined plan of action, Adiang had resolved to change his circumstances and, above all, to uplift his parents, especially his beloved Nyanti, from the struggles of the ghetto. The indomitable spirit of our children, their capacity to remember, and their unwavering determination to transform a situation from nothing to something, even without any apparent means, can only be attributed to their faith in God. This is why we hold on to the belief in miracles, for without it, some of the events in our lives would seem unjustifiably remarkable.

> "Satan wants you to focus on your lack instead of abundance. Adam and Eve had to pass by all of their abundance and disregarded it to get to the things they lacked. Focus on your abundance, not your lack."
>
> – *Nyanti*

7

Tragedy Strikes

Amidst the chaos and beauty of Luanda's sprawling coastal strip, Adiang and a handful of fellow escapees found themselves in the capital city of Angola after many arduous attempts to leave the diamond fields of Lunda Norte. Luanda's aerial view was nothing short of spectacular, a breathtaking stretch where the land met the sea, adorned with administrative buildings, hotels, and financial institutions, including national and commercial banks. Yet, this mesmerizing beauty coexisted with the turmoil and upheaval brought about by the war, a city teeming with a blend of "regresados" (those who returned home from foreign countries after the war) and individuals who had left their hometowns in search of a better life in Luanda.

Adiang stood there, utterly speechless, amidst the visible juxtaposition of what could only be described as beauty and chaos, a situation created by the influx of people from the interior cities fleeing the war. Luanda, originally not built to accommodate such a vast population, now grappled with the consequences: homelessness, socioeconomic challenges, and political rivalries among the major parties of UNITA, MPLA, and FNLA.

The cityscape, dotted with tall buildings devoid of lights, resembled a daily marathon of physical exertion for its residents. They climbed and descended multiple flights of stairs, embarking on a quest for large gallons of water, which they hauled up to their apartments, some as high as the 12th floor and beyond.

"NACAO CORAGEM," or "Courageous Nation," was the name of the TV show that revolved around the post-war events, all unfolding at Independence Square, nestled at the base of the towering monument dedicated to the late father of Angolan independence, Agostinho Neto, in Luanda. Adiang and his friends found themselves directed to this bustling town square in search of help to reunite with their dispersed families. Appearing on this globally televised show, in collaboration with networks from various European, American, and other countries, offered them a glimmer of hope that their families might catch a glimpse of them and learn of their whereabouts.

After an interview, Adiang was guided to the neighborhood of Martyrs de Kifangondo, a well-known area in Luanda predominantly dominated by Congolese residents. It also boasted a significant presence of individuals from West, South, and Central Africa who engaged in lucrative businesses in the city.

A Reunion of Tears and Hope

Accompanied by his Congolese friend, who spoke French, Adiang sought assistance from a Malian merchant. This merchant was the proud owner of a unique phone booth for international calls, where Congolese residents often negotiated their calls in exchange for tiny diamond stones.

It had been seven long months since Adiang had been separated from his family, and as he fumbled with the phone numbers, he finally managed to connect with the childhood friend and classmate he had been searching for—Elvis. However, Elvis's mother initially seemed unaware of the caller's identity. As she called her son to the phone, Elvis recognized his friend's voice and joyously exclaimed, "Lii Chase!"

Adiang's close friends had affectionately nicknamed him "Lii Chase," a moniker inspired by his love for reading the books and novels of author James Hadley Chase. Though the exact meaning of the nickname remained a mystery to others, it held a special significance known only to Adiang and his friends.

Adiang listened intently on the other end of the line as the noise in Elvis's house grew louder, drowning their conversation in a tumultuous sea of emotions. Elvis couldn't believe that the voice on the phone belonged to his missing friend, given the rumors of Adiang's death in the Angolan war and various other stories circulating back home. As Adiang urgently inquired about his family and implored Elvis to help him locate his mother, he received the heartbreaking news of his father and senior brother's tragic passing.

Sitting on the dusty floor, Adiang wept uncontrollably. However, his Congolese friend, affectionately referred to as "moto na ngai," tapped him on the shoulder and alerted him to someone who wanted to speak to him. With reluctance, Adiang rose to his feet and returned to the cabin.

On the other end of the line, Nyanti's feeble voice crackled with uncertainty as she questioned the caller's identity. Adiang replied with "na me," meaning "it is me" in Pidgin English. Nyanti, having believed her son to be deceased in the Angolan war, requested that he speak in their dialect to confirm his identity.

As Adiang began speaking in their native dialect, the phone suddenly went dead, and he panicked. Elvis's voice reemerged on the line, delivering the unsettling message that "reme don collapse," or "Mom has fainted."

A heavy silence ensued, and Adiang's anxiety surged. After approximately 30 agonizing minutes of waiting, Nyanti's sobs and prayers resonated through the phone. In the background, neighbors could be heard shouting and exclaiming, "He is alive! He is alive!"

There was no time to recount the full story of his experiences at that moment. Adiang promised to call back another day but assured them that he was safe and in the capital city, where the ravages of war had not yet reached.

In the subsequent days, Adiang learned of his father's demise after a prolonged illness that had left him bedridden. His father had inquired about him daily until his final moments, believing his son to be lost in the war. Tragically, his senior brother had succumbed to complications from yellow fever, aggravated by the absence of proper medical care—a double blow of sorrow and loss that Adiang carried in his heart.

> God's favor in your life doesn't always begin with laughter. The angel told Mary, 'You are favored among women,' yet what followed for Mary was a series of controversies and pain. Favor can start with endurance and tears, but it is still favor. Avoid drawing quick conclusions.

— *Nyanti*

8

Sold into Slavery

A despicable, horrific, and eerie post-war atmosphere had engulfed the border city of Ouessou in the Congo Brazzaville as Adiang and Chimolo Pem made their way along the unique main road leading to the local airport. Abandoned houses, ravaged by the war, were strewn across the landscape. Elderly men and women, many with babies in tow, remained behind, unable to undertake the journey to Brazzaville where the promise of peace and a better life beckoned.

Seated inside the aircraft, Adiang and his companion Chimolo couldn't help but reflect on the perilous alternative they had narrowly avoided by not boarding the wooden boats used to traverse the treacherous waters of the Congo River. This river was infested with crocodiles and hippopotamuses, making it a deadly passage.

A Chadian woman they had encountered on the flight came to their aid. She generously offered them lodging at her premises and assisted in organizing the necessary documentation for the boys to continue their journey to South Africa. She emphasized that there was no way to reach their desired destination without passing through Angola.

Perilous Passage To Cabinda

Cabinda, an island province, is embroiled in a brutal war, fighting for its separation from Angola. This conflict significantly complicates and adds risk to the journey to Cabinda, the city the boys must reach to catch a military flight into the capital Luanda. The news of kidnappers demanding ransom forces the boys to delay their journey and seek an alternative route to Namibia. Unfortunately, their new path takes them through Zaire, the nation ruled by Mobutu Sese Seko, which is now known as the Democratic Republic of Congo. This new route feels like starting the journey all over again, and it's both costly and dangerous, given that another war is raging in this country.

After two weeks of careful consideration, the boys decide to face the reality and venture into Cabinda. However, this decision comes with some safeguards. They are accompanied by a police officer provided by the Chadian lady who has been assisting them. This officer accompanies them all the way into Cabinda. Along the journey through the forest from the Congo to Cabinda, they encounter various militant groups, including the FNLA, as well as military checkpoints. These groups often demand money to allow passage. If travelers can't pay, they may be left behind to work as forced labor, while the vehicle continues its journey without them.

The Cabinda Military airport is bustling with military veterans preparing to depart for Luanda early in the morning.

This flight is typically free for members of the Angolan military and veterans, some of whom have suffered amputations due to the war. They are returning home to reunite with their families in Luanda.

For a fee of $50, the boys gain access to the airport and blend in with the veterans, finding seats on the flight. Most of the pilots and planes are of Russian origin, with a few Portuguese and a significant number of Angolan military officials overseeing operations. These are aging Antonov aircraft used for both commercial and military purposes during this wartime period.

The departure is chaotic, with passengers and crew jostling in a disorganized manner after military officials have boarded. Some passengers even sit on the aircraft's floor when it becomes overcrowded. The noise generated by the aircraft is akin to an old village bus, and as the journey progresses, passengers pray fervently for a safe arrival. The flight is rife with tension and fear, and landing feels like a collision between the tarmac and the aircraft, followed by a thunderous applause from the relieved crew and passengers. They quickly disembark, fearing a potential explosion.

A Risky Escape Plan

It is the 11th of November, and the country is celebrating its Independence. As the passengers form a unique line towards the checkout, Adiang couldn't help but notice that the airport was infested with soldiers carrying all sorts of machine guns, pistols, and Kalashnikovs. In fact, the boys had never seen this type of arsenal before. Some of the soldiers appeared to be very young, and they were wrapped with bullets all over their bodies, carrying machine guns that were apparently bigger and heavier than their own weights.

Chimolo called Adiang aside, and they had to figure out a means to get out of this airport, just as they had entered Cabinda. The situation grew worse as they were ushered along with a machine gun-wielding soldier to follow the line. Everyone was speaking Portuguese, and the boys felt lost without a word of Portuguese. Chimolo decided to follow the line, while Adiang fumbled and pretended he had left his luggage inside the aircraft. He rushed back to collect it, and on his return, Chimolo had been handcuffed and escorted into an alley.

Adiang hid behind the door that separated the entry into the hallway and the tarmac. Suddenly, he felt a tap on his shoulder, and fear surged through him as a soldier demanded his papers in Portuguese. Adiang replied in English and told the soldier that he was Namibian and needed to leave the airport. It turned out that the soldier spoke English and demanded money to help him get out.

Adiang accepted the offer and got into the trunk of the military car after negotiating with a Colonel who promised to also help Chimolo, who was now under arrest. Nobody knew what they planned to do with him. When the trunk was finally opened after what seemed like hours, Adiang could hardly believe the new reality he was facing.

> We become what we think. Our thoughts become our intentions, our intentions become our actions, our actions become our habits, our habits become our second nature, and our second nature becomes our identity. So, take good care of your thoughts, for we become what we think.

— *Nyanti*

9

The Diamond Fields of Angola

It has been 7 months since Adiang landed in Lunda Norte, and it was only recently that he heard the name of the province for the first time. Under the control of UNITA guerillas, diamond smuggling activities between the Angolan province of Lunda Norte and the neighboring Congolese city of Kasai had been ongoing since 1980 until the early 2000s. These activities contributed significantly to the dollarization of both nations' economies. The national currencies of both countries had lost significance as dollars were used everywhere on a daily basis, thanks to the large amounts generated by diamond smuggling. This led to the transformation of villages into bustling diamond settlements, attracting a great influx of Americans and Europeans in search of diamonds.

Meanwhile, Luanda, the capital city of Angola, is the location where the bloody and prolonged process of independence began. On the 4th of January 1961, when a protest for just and better agricultural wages grew into a violent demonstration that spread to the northern region of the country, a brutal response by the Portuguese military repressed the rebellion.

This marked the awakening and resurgence of much-needed Angolan nationalism, which also anticipated the difficulties confronted by the independence movement.

The following years witnessed the emergence of different fronts and independence movements all over Angola. The FNLA, which pioneered the movement in 1961, was formed in the northern region, mainly comprising people from the BAKONGO ethnic group.

Diamonds smuggled in Angola.

The MPLA, a Marxist and Leninist group formed by Angolan intellectuals in Luanda, gained power. Meanwhile, UNITA, composed mostly of defectors from the FNLA, gathered strength and consolidated its presence around the central region of the country within the OVIMBUNDU ethnic group. In the next decade, each of these groups confronted the Portuguese military and paramilitary forces, financed by Portugal.

Due to their ideological and ethnic differences, each of these groups fought independently, and as a result, none of them succeeded in defeating Portugal. In 1974, the Portuguese forces pushed these factions to their limits, and in an unexpected turn of events, Portugal underwent a military coup on April 25, 1974. With the end of the colonial regime, the interest in maintaining African colonies disappeared. After 400 years, the colonial period in Angola came to an abrupt and brutal end. Nevertheless, the ethnic and ideological divisions persisted. The MPLA took control of the capital city, expelling the FNLA from Luanda and appointing AGOSTINHO NETO as the new President of the Republic of Angola.

This marked the first step toward a civil war that would extend for decades. The conflict assumed an international dimension, with millions of Cuban soldiers and Yugoslavian warships supporting the Marxist-Leninist MPLA group, while South Africa, former ZAIRE (Democratic Republic of Congo), and the United States provided secret financing to support the FNLA and UNITA, who eventually formed an alliance. Amid the backdrop of the Cold War, the Angolan territory became a battleground between the MPLA and UNITA in various battles over the years, with various foreign powers strengthening the capacities of both sides to continue fighting.

Despite temporary ceasefires and failed negotiations, the war persisted into the 70s and 80s, and neither side could secure a decisive victory. With the end of the Cold War, the Angolan civil war lost its ideological and international appeal. President JOSE EDUARDO DOS SANTOS, who took over from President NETO after his death in 1979, liberalized the Angolan economy, while UNITA continued to finance its war effort through the diamond trade. However, as sanctions against the diamond trade became increasingly stringent with the end of the Cold War, UNITA found it increasingly difficult to secure funding to continue the fight. Consequently, the Angolan civil war finally came to an end in 2002 with the death of UNITA's leader. After nearly 30 years of conflict, peace negotiations commenced.

In the midst of the tropical forest, a vast and extensive landscape with numerous excavations resembled dormant volcanoes. These were man-made craters, the result of the massive industry of illegal diamond exploration, entirely controlled by UNITA guerillas. A small group of 25 men, both young and old, were held hostage as they worked day in and day out in the illegal mines, searching for diamonds. Large, deep holes were dug into the ground, where the strongest men in the group descended with shovels, axes, and spades, using whatever tools could facilitate the digging process. The excavated soil was placed into buckets, held by ropes, and then pulled up to the surface. Other miners had the task of passing the soil through a locally made machine to separate the stones from the soil, using water, and then putting the diamonds into thick black bags that were later stored in the warehouse.

Some of these excavation holes were so large and deep that merely looking into them from the top gave the impression of a free fall. Descending these steep and watery valleys in circles was made possible with the help of very strong ropes attached to iron poles at the top and bottom of the valley. Miners had to hold onto the ropes while descending or climbing the valley.

Once in the valley, they dug from sunrise to sunset, with only a 1-hour break, which was later reduced to 45 minutes after an incident occurred.

The mixture of rocky terrain and thick brown earth made descending and climbing these slippery, watery, and swirling excavations challenging, significantly slowing down the work rhythm. This is why the so-called "rope technology" was invented by the one and only overseer, popularly known as Capitao do Mato, or "Bush Captain." Always dressed in his charismatic and decorated military uniform, he single-handedly controlled his crew and its workers in a deadly slave labor environment.

The Deadly Discovery

Ngunza was approximately 19 years old when he was forcibly brought into the camp, along with his three siblings, who primarily spoke the Kwanyama dialect.

It was precisely 12 noon, with the scorching sun directly overhead, making it too hot for anyone to work. Capitao do Mato disliked repeating his orders, and it was time for the shift change. Ngunza began his descent down the slope towards the digging site, his grip firm on the rope. However, in an attempt to steady himself against the steep wall, he lost his balance and tumbled down onto the hard soil, lifeless.

Despite attempts at mouth-to-mouth resuscitation and CPR, Ngunza remained lifeless and was declared dead on the spot by Capitao do Mato. Due to the extreme heat, empty stomachs, and Ngunza's exhaustion, he had fainted while descending into the excavation pit. Capitao do Mato wasted no time in conducting a ruthless search for diamonds on Ngunza's lifeless body.

Ngunza had a habit of constantly chewing dried meat, which the Captain despised and questioned. The Captain held a personal grudge against Ngunza and his siblings because they hailed from a different tribe, one considered traitorous during the Angolan liberation war. In response, Ngunza explained that the meat was a mixture of medicinal plants and thin male goat skin, providing energy to shepherds during long journeys to feed their flocks without tiring.

Seated atop the lifeless body, Capitao do Mato struggled to open Ngunza's mouth and was shocked to find a thread-like string inside. Slowly, it revealed a small nylon bag filled with well-preserved diamond stones hidden in the dead man's belly. Next, the Captain turned his attention to Ngunza's anus, using an iron rod like a surgeon to explore the depths. Capitao do Mato, a towering figure with dark sunglasses that shielded his eyes even in darkness, was feared by all. He did not hesitate to execute those who crossed him, and the forest, seemingly boundless, served as his dominion.

He often reminded everyone that they were free to run but would get nowhere, and if caught, they would not live to tell the tale. The forest was their open prison, where escape was futile, and the consequences for attempting it were clear:

either death at the hands of the Captain or a gruesome end at the claws of the wild animals that roamed the camp's periphery.

The camp is an abandoned UNHCR Refugee camp taken over by the UNITA rebels. A few tents with the symbols of the UNHCR have been adapted with tarpaulin bags to withstand the rain and the sun in both seasons that dominate this part of Africa. Lined up amidst the bushes are the few tents that serve as homes to the miners, with three men in each tent, totaling 15 tents.

An artist's impression of the beatings of the slaves.

Nighttime was the time for reflection and discussion about the future, which was very doubtful yet not impossible for those who believed. The miners took turns at the fireside, which illuminated the forest and kept wild animals at bay. Adiang always held his rosary close to him as he stared directly into the fire. He remembered that no one knew his whereabouts, and if he died here, nobody would ever find his body, and he would have never existed. This was quite an unbelievable situation, and he always refused to let his mind dwell on such thoughts. Prayers took place in the middle of the night when the Captain and his "capangas" (crew) were fast asleep. The fire represented hope for many here, especially for Adiang, who saw it burning inside him—the dream that had prompted him to leave his family, friends, and home for greener pastures. This dream couldn't end here, he thought to himself. The fire now symbolized hope for a future beyond this hellfire, igniting a bigger fire within him for freedom and safety, which were what really mattered at this point in time.

Food was served promptly at exactly 2 pm, which also marked the 45-minute allocated break time. Today's menu was the first of its kind, as the Captain was celebrating the sale of a significant quantity of diamonds to expatriate Europeans from Johannesburg. Funge and Makayabo, locally made specialties, were served on rubber plates. As the military men consumed scotch whisky and smoked Cuban cigars and marijuana, they closely monitored their slaves to identify anyone who wasn't happy.

It's important to mention that any discord or misconduct from the slaves was met with severe punishment at the so-called "tronco," a tree where their hands were handcuffed around it, and they were whipped on their backs. They couldn't defend themselves and had to endure the pain in a static position. The soldiers would invade the neighboring villages once a month for livestock. They would brutally kidnap and rape the women whom they forced to cook food and kill the men who could not serve as slaves to dig the diamonds.

For a young man who, just a few days ago, was enjoying freedom in a relatively democratic nation, finding himself in a completely opposite and extremely dangerous situation like this was surreal for Adiang. Sometimes, he would awaken in the middle of the night, thinking it was a nightmare, but it wasn't. This was his new reality, a bitter pill to swallow. However, the Bible says, "Faith is the substance of things hoped for, the evidence of things not seen," and so Adiang clung firmly to these words, keeping his silent prayers with a steadfast belief that change would come soon.

In such dire circumstances, faith alone wasn't enough to survive in this jungle; obedience to the laws stipulated by the Captain was paramount. There was no manual to read or memorize the laws that governed slave life, but one had to rely on memory to retain and adhere to whatever the Captain declared as law in the forest. Observing every detail, especially body movements, became crucial because the Captain was a man of few words, and one could often discern his intentions from his actions. Adiang had honed his ability to perceive people to a high degree due to the ever-present fear of death or the "Tronco" (Guillotine).

Under the massive Baobab tree, locally known as "Imbondeiro," surrounded by large sack-cloths and a roughly tailored tarpaulin roof, stood the Captain's house, which also served as the diamond warehouse. It was an unbreakable rule that no one, under any circumstance, should approach this side of the forest; the penalty was instant death, and nobody dared to defy it.

Gunshots are heard not far from the camp, and panic takes control of all the slaves. They know full well that in the case of an invasion, they can consider themselves as dead people, as the new commanders wipe out everything and everyone to conquer the new territory. Trying to run into the bushes, Adiang and the rest are held at gunpoint as the military trucks drive into the camp, still spraying bullets in the air.

Contrary to the filthy but charismatic Captain, "Pai Grande" BIG DADDY is a physically fit, tiny, and staunchly vicious-looking Military General who operates the jungle without mercy. The general is affectionately called as such for his dreaded and merciless deeds during the war. The great and mighty man of war, as some call him, the General is very tactful in his moves and words when addressing the crowd. His camouflage uniform has no distinction and is very clean. His red beret reminds one of the Argentinian/Cuban Revolutionary fighter Che Guevara. His boots are as shiny as a mirror, and one can only question how he maintains this stature in the midst of all the chaos in the land. One can only draw one conclusion: the fight is the mindset. His physical appearance and cleanliness show how mentally ready he is to go forward in this war. His environment doesn't affect his mindset in any way, as his convictions are beyond his present situation and struggles.

Adiang observes the General with a peculiar mix of disdain and admiration for his personality and character. There is without a doubt something to be learned from this man. The obstacles in life should never change your perception of life; they only come to build you and make you stronger for the future. Without these obstacles, you will surely be unprepared for the future blessings. Life is not just the passing of time; it is a collection of experiences, their frequency, and intensity. Whatever the span of your life turns out to be, fill it up with experiences and the intensity of those experiences. It is never too young to die if you've lived a life filled with experiences and their intensity.

The General was an eloquent example of such a person, and in an awkward way, Adiang felt to some extent that he wanted to be just like the General because he inspired trust in himself, courage, faith, and a desire to be the best or a reference to many. It is known that anything can happen during any war, but the way he lived his life made him look fearless. Instead of fear, the war made him appear very confident, almost like a God walking the earth.

There will be seasons in your life where God's grace will be proven by the fire you go through. Whenever God has a great purpose in your life, He will put a great problem in front of you. Goliath was the gateway to the next dimension for David. If not for Goliath, David would still be taking care of the sheep. The same goes for Joseph, who saw himself sold by his brothers as a slave but ended up becoming the prime minister of Egypt and saving his family from hunger.

Some of us at some point in our lives think our greatest acquisitions are behind us, but we're wrong. You've made it out of all odds alive, but I tell you that what's behind you is your training, and the greatest victories of your life are ahead of you.

> "If you're free, your responsibility is to free somebody else. If you have power, your duty is to empower somebody else."
>
> – *Nyanti*

10

The Digging for Life Paradigm

Like Adiang, you may find yourself in a situation where you're *"Digging For Life"*. Life's path often takes unexpected turns, and sometimes, we're thrust into challenging circumstances as we navigate toward our destinies. Adiang, driven by a simple yet profound desire for a better life for himself and his family, found himself in an unlikely place—the diamond fields of Angola, where he embarked on a different kind of journey, one of literal and metaphorical digging. Let's unpack the concept of *"Digging for Life,"* exploring the profound lessons hidden beneath the earth's surface and deep within ourselves.

In the pursuit of a meaningful and fulfilling existence, we often find ourselves on a journey of self-discovery. This journey, encapsulated in the idea of *"Digging for Life,"* is a process that moves individuals into an authentic relationship with themselves, by themselves, for themselves, and ultimately, for the betterment of humanity.

"Digging for Life" begins with the acknowledgment that authenticity is the cornerstone of personal growth. It's about embracing your true self, unearthing the layers of conditioning

and societal expectations that may have accumulated over time. It involves confronting your fears, your doubts, and your insecurities head-on. This process is not about conforming to external standards but rather about recognizing and celebrating your unique identity.

The Power of Positivity

In our quest for authenticity, we encounter challenges that test our resolve. It is during these moments that the concept of "offensive positivity" comes into play. To be offensively positive means to choose positivity as an unwavering stance, regardless of circumstances or external influences. It's the understanding that the most significant battle you'll ever face is the one within yourself. By maintaining a positive outlook and an unshakable belief in your abilities, you fortify yourself for the journey ahead.

The Transformational Power of Action

Transformation begins when you take action. Change only occurs when you decide to change, and this decision is often accompanied by the willingness to endure discomfort and tackle challenges head-on. *"Digging for Life"* implies that if you choose the easy path, your life will inevitably be fraught with difficulties. However, if you summon the courage to undertake the harder, more rewarding challenges, your life will ultimately become more manageable and fulfilling.

Clarity and Goal Setting

Clarity is the compass that guides us on our path. When you are crystal clear about what you want, where you're headed, and who you want to become, your mind becomes a powerful ally in achieving your aspirations. It's as if the universe conspires to assist you when you have a clear vision of your goals. The more specific and vivid your goals are, the faster your mind can chart the course to reach them.

Crafting Your Authentic Performance

With reference to any life path, you choose, consider the six principles of Stanislavski's method—an approach renowned for crafting emotionally expressive and authentic performances in the realm of acting. Through meticulous preparation and rehearsals, this method encourages actors to internalize their character's inner self, understanding their motivations and emotional states on a profound level.

In the grand production of life, we are all the actors of our own narratives. Just as in acting, the authenticity and depth of our character representation can make all the difference. How connected are you to your goals? Are you fully immersed in the role you play on your life's stage? It's not enough to be a mere performer; you must also become the writer, producer, director, and the lead actor of your own script.

Stanislavski's six essential questions, which actors employ to delve into their roles, can serve as guiding principles in any field, helping you navigate the path to your aspirations:

WHO - Who am I? Understanding your core identity is the first step in aligning your actions with your authentic self.

WHAT - What are my objectives? What are my goals, and what steps am I taking to achieve them?

WHY - Why am I here? Why am I pursuing this particular goal? What is the driving force behind my actions?

WHEN - When do I begin, and when do I expect to reach the finish line? Timing is key in executing your plans.

WHERE - Where do I come from, and where am I headed? Understanding your roots and your destination can provide valuable context for your journey.

HOW - The process, the intricate steps you take, is what brings your goals to fruition. Mastery of this process is mastery of life itself.

Remember, the price you pay and the prize you win at the end of your journey will be a direct reflection of your dedication and commitment. Mastering the creative process is akin to mastering the natural process of succeeding in life. Approach it with creativity and passion, for this is your life's most significant project, and there are no second chances.

Adiang's Lessons: Keys to Succeed at Digging for Life

Adiang's life and story teach us many profound lessons. Life is a complex and unpredictable journey, and sometimes the pursuit of greatness can be a double-edged sword. It's essential to recognize that greatness often comes with its own set of challenges. In the crucible of his experiences, we uncover valuable keys to success in the art of *"Digging for Life."*

1. **Sometimes being great isn't so great.** Greatness is not always glamorous. It can mean facing immense pressure, expectations, and responsibilities. It's about acknowledging that the path to success may be arduous, but the rewards can be worth the struggle.

2. **Sometimes being great means being crushed and not allowed to whimper.** In the pursuit of our dreams, there may be moments when we feel overwhelmed, when life seems to be testing our limits. These are the times when we must summon our inner strength and resilience, for it's in these crucibles that true greatness is forged.

3. **Sometimes bearing that you're in a crushing season and yet helping other people and going home alone to empty yourself.** Greatness often involves self-sacrifice. It means extending a helping hand to others even when facing personal challenges. It's about understanding that your ability to uplift others can be a source of strength in itself, even when you return home to your own battles.

4. **Encourage others along the way.** The act of supporting and inspiring others can be draining, but it's also a testament to your character. In these moments of vulnerability, remember that it's okay to seek solace and find ways to rejuvenate your own spirit.

5. **Setting your priorities right and learning to say no.** Greatness requires discernment. It's about setting clear priorities and learning when to say no to distractions that don't align with your goals. This self-discipline is essential for maintaining focus.

6. **Discipline is freedom, Indiscipline is prison.** Discipline is not a restriction but a path to liberation. It provides the structure and consistency needed to achieve greatness. When you discipline yourself, you create the space and freedom to pursue your aspirations.

7. **Confidence comes from preparation.** Confidence isn't an innate trait but a product of thorough preparation and knowledge. When you invest the time and effort in honing your skills and expertise, confidence naturally follows.

8. **Knowing how great you are.** Recognize your own greatness. Understand that you possess the potential to achieve remarkable things. Self-belief is the cornerstone of any successful journey.

9. **Gratitude for the privilege of being alive.** Life itself is a gift, and every day is an opportunity to embrace your journey. The realization of this privilege can be a powerful motivator to make the most of each moment.

10. **When you focus on improving yourself, victory will come to you.** Victory is a by-product of self-improvement. Instead of fixating on the end goal, focus on becoming the best version of yourself. Victory will naturally gravitate toward your efforts.

11. **You attract based on who you are, not what you want.** Your character and actions define the opportunities and people you attract into your life. To attract positivity and success, work on improving yourself from within.

12. **Don't chase... attract.** Instead of chasing success, cultivate an environment where success is drawn to you. This shift in mindset can lead to more sustainable achievements.

13. **You are the best.** Embrace a positive self-affirmation. Tell yourself that you are the best, not out of arrogance but as a declaration of self-worth and confidence.

14. **You can't do it alone.** While self-reliance is valuable, don't hesitate to seek support when needed. The journey to greatness often involves collaboration and learning from others.

15. **God is always with you.** For those with faith, the belief that a higher power is guiding their path can provide strength and comfort during challenging times.

16. **Today is your day.** Every day brings new opportunities and possibilities. Embrace each day with the belief that it holds the potential for significant progress and achievements.

17. **Adopt a winning mindset.** Even in the face of setbacks, view yourself as a winner who learns and grows from every experience.

18. **Sometimes you need to be knocked down before you figure out what your fight is and how you need to fight it.** Adversity can reveal your true purpose and the unique battles you are meant to face. It's often through challenges that your inner strength and purpose are activated.

19. **Sometimes you need to feel the pain of defeat to activate the real passion and purpose that God predestined inside you.** Defeat can be a catalyst for profound personal growth. It ignites the passion and purpose that may have been dormant, propelling you toward your destined path.

20. **God has plans for your prosperity.** Embrace the knowledge that the plans God has for you are not meant to harm, but rather to prosper and provide hope for a brighter future. Even in the face of uncertainty, trust in His divine guidance.

21. **When one door closes, find the open window.** In times of disappointment and closed doors, shift your focus from what's behind you to what lies ahead. Opportunities often present themselves in unexpected ways—look for the open window.

22. **Tomorrow starts today.** Successful people understand that planning their day the night before is a key to productivity. It allows you to start each day with purpose and direction, ready to tackle your goals.

23. **Anger is self-inflicted emotion.** Realize that anger is often an emotional punishment you impose on yourself in response to someone else's behavior. Learning to manage and redirect this emotion is a valuable skill on your journey.

24. **Embrace life's dualities**. Acknowledge that the gift of existence comes with its fair share of suffering. Gratitude for both the joys and the challenges of life allows you to fully appreciate the beauty of your existence.

25. **You are destined for greatness.** Hold fast to the belief that you are destined for greatness, even when life takes unexpected detours. These diversions are part of your unique journey, shaping you into the person you are meant to be.

26. **Embrace the power of singular focus.** Understand that the path to success often involves unwavering dedication to a single idea. To achieve greatness, immerse yourself in your chosen pursuit, leaving no room for distraction.

27. **Be committed to your dreams.** Be prepared to endure loneliness, depression, disrespect, laughter, lost friendships, failures, and neglect when you are resolute about your life's purpose. Your unwavering commitment will see you through.

28. **Know your worth.** Never allow anyone to diminish your sense of self-worth. You are valuable, and your journey is significant, regardless of others' opinions.

29. **Become more than you are.** Recognize that you can achieve more in life by continually striving to become more than you currently are. Personal growth is the key to expanding your horizons.

30. **Acknowledge the source always.** Remember to praise God, the ultimate source of all blessings. While people may be channels of support, they are not the ultimate source. Keep your faith grounded, even as you appreciate the help of others.

31. **Do the right thing despite the odds.** *"Digging for Life"* means being willing to do the right thing, even when faced with daunting challenges and obstacles. It's a commitment to integrity and moral fortitude.

32. **Make the world better than you found it.** As you embark on your journey of self-discovery and growth, remember that *"Digging for Life"* also involves contributing positively to the world around you. Strive to leave a lasting, positive impact.

33. **Become a servant for others' goals.** *"Digging for Life"* extends to serving others in their pursuits. Act as a guide and support for those striving to reach their own goals, fostering a sense of community and mutual growth.

34. **Lift others to the top.** Part of *"Digging for Life"* is recognizing the power of lifting others to their full potential. When you empower and elevate those around you, you contribute to a collective journey toward success.

When someone asks you, "What are you doing?" respond with pride and conviction: I am *"Digging for Life."* It's a declaration of your commitment to self-discovery, growth, and making a meaningful impact on the world.

> "Great people aren't born great, they grow into greatness."
>
> — *Nyanti*

Part 3

ESCAPE AND REDEMPTION

> In order for something new to emerge, something old must fade away. Sometimes, letting go of all you've known and grown accustomed to is necessary. Never fear starting anew because what's been obstructed can be revived.

— Nyanti

11

A Divine Intervention

Camama cemetery, situated on the outskirts of Luanda along the road leading to the Viana municipality, is not just an ordinary graveyard. It serves multiple purposes, extending beyond its role as a final resting place. Adiang found himself here after leaving the "Ponto de Reencontro" (The Meeting Point), where countless families gathered daily in search of lost loved ones. It was also a place for those wishing to send signals to family and friends worldwide, signaling their survival through the presence of media reporters, marking the end of a long and brutal war.

In the heart of Luanda, lies the famous Bairro dos Operários, a neighborhood predominantly inhabited by impoverished families living in multicolored apartment houses. The neighborhood's charm shifted with the seasons, as muddy and dusty roads influenced the colors of the buildings. Adiang shared a one-bedroom apartment with his Congolese friend, Moto na Ngai, who had managed to escape the war with a handful of diamonds. Moto's plan was simple: sell the diamonds and find his way back to the Congo Republic. He sought potential buyers among the neighborhood's older residents, hoping they might know someone interested.

But then, the piercing sound of gunshots shattered the neighborhood's fragile peace. Five heavily armed men descended upon Adiang, forcibly restraining him, and flinging him into the back of a police truck. His home was ransacked, and the men, identifying themselves as criminal investigators from the "DINIC" (National Criminal Investigation Department), drove Adiang to the police headquarters in Luanda. There, he endured daily beatings, pressured to reveal the whereabouts of his comrade, Moto na Ngai, and the stolen diamonds.

After two grueling weeks at the DINIC building, Adiang was cast into prison by the prosecutor, who failed to find any evidence of the diamonds. Comarca Prison, situated on the outskirts of Luanda along the road to Cacuacu, was surrounded by a formidable brick cement wall, isolating it from the main highway that traversed Luanda, connecting to neighboring cities. The prison, encased in heavy concrete and iron bars, was designed to deter any escape attempts. The prison guards, clad in brown khaki uniforms, maintained relentless vigilance, subjecting visitors to rigorous entry and exit procedures. The faded brown and yellow paint on the prison walls hinted at a stern and unyielding institution. Adiang found an unexpected sense of relief within the confines of Comarca, as the state prosecutor, in an attempt to avoid human rights scrutiny, had effectively sentenced him to spend the rest of his days behind bars.

Comarca Jail

Comarca jail is one of the largest and most overcrowded jails in Luanda. Within its walls, from the most sinister felons to the ordinary thieves, souls were shackled by their misdeeds. Each Cazerna, a sector of this vast prison, housed inmates based on the nature of their transgressions.

On one fateful day, the DINIC van, a symbol of dread for many, arrived, carrying 11 souls. Their eyes were shielded by blindfolds, ensuring that the path to Comarca remained a mystery. This was a preventive measure, a strategy to hinder any thoughts of escape. As they disembarked, they were lined up, like pawns in a cruel game, in the courtyard. When the blindfolds were removed, the sun's glare momentarily blinded them. Slowly, as their sight returned, the daunting walls of Comarca loomed, reminiscent of the legendary Fort Boyard off the French coast.

Soon after, the chiefs of the Cazernas were summoned. Their task was to select the newcomers for their respective sectors. Among the arrivals was Adiang, a foreigner destined for Cazerna 4, under the watchful eye of its leader, Mr. Christopher, or as he was affectionately known, Christopher Alleluia.

The guards, with their piercing gazes, escorted the prisoners to their new homes. For Adiang, the initiation was swift. Seated on the cold, unforgiving cement floor, the rules of the prison echoed in his ears. The customs of the Cazerna were clear: newcomers bore the burden of maintaining the lavatory's cleanliness. And so, Adiang's first nights were spent in this very place, a rite of passage for all fresh inmates, sleeping amidst the overpowering stench of shit.

The walls of Cazerna 4 bore silent witnesses to its history, etched in graffiti and paintings, each telling a tale of past inhabitants. Christopher Alleluia's chamber was distinct, serving multiple purposes: a sleeping quarter, a courtroom, and an investigation hub. Here, when Adiang's body gave in to the overwhelming stench of shit, a trial was held.

It was a challenging start for Adiang. Each dawn, he was faced with the task of cleaning the vast lavatory, a space of merely 4x4 meters yet catering to countless inmates. His tools? An old rag and minimal water. The process was grueling: cleaning, lifting the pit covers, and then, with a dish, transferring the waste to a basin. The final step was to carry this basin, balanced precariously on his head, to a pit behind the prison, overlooking the cacuacu streets.

Morning showers were a brief respite, taken in shifts within a narrow chamber adorned with a pole that sporadically sprayed water. But this relief was short-lived, for by 8 am, the tap would run dry, only to be revived the next dawn.

Ill In Prison

In the dimly lit cell of Comarca, as dawn broke, the prisoners' chatters and grunts were overshadowed by a conspicuous silence. Adiang, who usually was up before the others, lay motionless. A couple of impatient slaps jolted him, accompanied by harsh words mocking his perceived laziness. But the true ailment was evident to any onlooker: his face swollen to a grotesque extent, eyes sealed shut, and wounds on his head oozing with a sinister shade.

The guards, sensing the gravity of the situation, swiftly carried him to the prison's rudimentary dispensary. Though they attempted to offer some relief, the severity of his condition demanded more specialized care. Thus, Adiang found himself transported to the renowned MARIA PIA hospital in Mutamba.

Upon his return, instead of rest, Adiang was thrust into the prison's courtroom. Whispers and accusations danced around him, with claims that his collapse was but a ruse to shirk his dreaded toilet cleaning duty. But medical reports, bearing the weight of undeniable evidence, painted a grim picture: prolonged exposure to the noxious fumes from the jail's toilets had wreaked havoc on his lungs.

In light of this revelation, Adiang was granted a small mercy. A thin mattress, layered with carbon papers, was allotted to him at the foot of the bed of the prison's most influential inmate, the head of Cazerna 4, known affectionately as Christopher

Alleluia. This gesture was symbolic, an unprecedented privilege. The prison was divided: the private sector, a realm for the seasoned prisoners who had earned their place through time and power dynamics, and the general sector, a vast hall with iron bunk beds and less fortunate souls sprawled on meager mattresses.

Christopher Alleluia's chamber was a testament to his stature. It was meticulously maintained, housing an array of documents, food, and gifts. The room was akin to a vault, safeguarding the possessions of other inmates, who feared theft. His authority was unparalleled, balancing a mix of reverence, fear, and justice. His ties with the prison guards and the superintendent were well-known, ensuring his influence permeated every corner of Comarca.

But even he wasn't exempt from the notorious "Cleaning Day." On this day, the basketball court became a holding area for all inmates while guards scoured the Cazernas. Discovery of any illicit item brought swift repercussions.

Recreation was a luxury, and the prison's makeshift futsal field served as an arena for fierce matches between Cazernas. Bets were placed fervently, with stakes ranging from cigarettes to clothing. Even the guards indulged in this vice. Talented players were sometimes "imported" for matches, discreetly brought in and out by the guards.

Basketball, though, was the crown jewel of sports in Angola. The nation, boasting accolades and renowned clubs like Petro de Luanda and Primeiro de Agosto, reveled in its status as Africa's basketball titan. And within the confines of Comarca, the echoes of this passion resonated just as loudly.

Breakthrough Behind bars

In the depths of Comarca, amidst the shadows and echoes of despair, some of us find ourselves. It's a paradox, really, that jail can be the crucible where we discover our true selves. In the solitude of confinement, whether by choice or necessity, you have the opportunity to embrace loneliness. It's in this isolation that you can unearth your hidden potential. His breakthtrough came from behind bars.

God speaks to us in myriad ways, often in the quiet moments when we're forced to listen. He yearns to reveal your inner strength and show you the unique gifts bestowed within you. The tunnel may seem endless, dark, and daunting, but remember, at the end of that tunnel, there's no doubt that light awaits. Open your mind, and listen closely to the whispers of destiny.

Adiang's story is a testament to this transformative power. He discovered his passion for filmmaking and acting while incarcerated, drawn into the mesmerizing world of Brazilian telenovelas. In the midst of his confinement, he had a dream, a vision that others might dismiss as mere fantasy. One night, bathed in sweat, he saw himself sharing the screen with the lead character, Caua Reymond, from the popular Brazilian sitcom "Malhação."

Remarkably, this dream turned into reality as he later starred in a TV show, "O CAÇADOR," alongside Caua Reymond in Brazil. It's a testament to the mysterious ways in which God unfolds our destinies. Sometimes, He takes us on unexpected journeys, like Joseph's tale from the Bible. Joseph's dreams of leadership led his jealous brothers to sell him into slavery, but ultimately, he became the governor of Egypt, a cornerstone that became the headstone.

So, as you read this, I implore you to listen to your intuition. God is speaking to someone through these words. Your dreams, no matter how grand or humble, matter. Don't let anyone define who you are or what you can achieve. You were created for greatness, and this is your time to shine.

For those of you who have been waiting for a sign, perhaps this is it. Don't wait any longer to chase your dreams. Life is made up of unforgettable moments, and in the end, it's these moments that truly matter. Material wealth fades away, but the memories and experiences you gather along the way are what truly define your legacy.

Talk to the love of your life, take the risk, pursue your passions, and live a life with no regrets. As you read these words, remember the wisdom of the old folks in your family and the stories of those on their dying beds. They, more than anyone, would tell you that the only true regret in life is not having lived it to the fullest. Seize this moment, for it is yours, and your dreams are waiting to be realized.

Miraculous Escape

Adiang had spent a month behind bars when, one day, his name echoed through the jail's corridors. In prison, the mere mention of one's name could signify various possibilities – transfer to another facility, a lawyer seeking contact, or the long-awaited release. Adiang had not encountered a lawyer since his arrival at Comarca jail, so he was taken aback by the unexpected announcement. Earlier that morning, a Congolese pastor had prophesied his release in a dream, but Adiang had presumed he was merely being relocated to another prison. However, as the guard instructed him to gather his belongings and announced his impending release, the unbelievable reality sank in.

Adiang had arrived in jail with nothing, and during his time there, he would bathe only at night, washing his clothes and drying them behind the massive fans located at the end of the building. These fans provided some relief to the overheated and overcrowded narrow corridors, as the jail's population had far exceeded its original capacity. Adiang dedicated a significant portion of his time in jail to the library, offering English language lessons to fellow inmates. As he rushed to express his gratitude and bid farewell to the pastor and his comrades, they shook hands and waved goodbye with genuine joy, acknowledging that he did not deserve to be there in the first place.

The sun beat down relentlessly, yet Adiang, who stood just beyond the jail gates, felt an abrupt chill. He was only a few steps away from the main road, which served as the boundary between the jail and the neighborhoods of Luanda. In the midst of savoring his newfound freedom, Adiang contemplated his next move. A sense of peace enveloped him as he settled beside a massive rock outside the jail, gazing out at the sprawling city of Luanda.

Across the road, a black van had been parked for some time. Adiang watched the ceaseless flow of vehicles along the streets of Cacuacu. Suddenly, a man disembarked from the van and signaled to Adiang. Assuming it was a free ride, or "Boleia" as it's called in Luanda, Adiang hurriedly approached the van, eager for a lift to downtown Luanda. As he drew closer, the man's face came into focus, a visage that haunted his memories and was the last person he wanted to encounter, even in his nightmares – Capitao do Mato.

Capitao do Mato held a semi-rifle in his hand and gestured for Adiang to enter the van. Stunned and speechless, Adiang felt an eerie compulsion, like a hypnotic trance. He mounted the van and took a seat beside two armed men who wasted no time in demanding, "Where is your partner in crime?" Stammering and bewildered, Adiang replied, "Who... What partner... What crime?"

Before he could finish his sentence, a brutal blow from a gun struck his face, causing blood to gush and splatter throughout the van. The second man brandished a military knife, intent on inflicting more harm. Adiang instinctively tried to defend himself, resulting in a scuffle within the confines of the van. The knife found its mark on his thigh, drawing blood. It was only when Capitao do Mato managed to intervene, averting a catastrophe, that the violence ceased. Adiang was bleeding profusely from all over his body and was immediately taken to an abandoned house, where he spent the entire day with some other individuals, all of them in handcuffs, anxiously awaiting the possibility of execution.

It was 3 AM in the morning when the van pulled up outside the Camama Cemetery in Luanda. The gates were opened and closed immediately after the van entered the cemetery. In the distance, some unidentified men were busy digging a grave and pushing human bodies inside, then covering them with soil. It began to dawn on Adiang that today might be his last day on planet Earth. He started singing in silence a song: ("A demain il fera beau sur la grande route A demain il fera beau sur le chemin Demain un jour nouveau Demain tous les oiseaux Chanteront sur la route demain...") which means "Tomorrow will be a new and better day; the birds will sing on the way..." while calling out the name "JESUS" incessantly.

As the guards were busy discussing how the execution and burial would happen, another van drove into the cemetery, and Moto na Ngai was thrown to the ground. He was unrecognizable, covered in blood, and his face swollen from multiple punches with the gun. Moto was in agonizing pain, and it seemed his jaw was broken as he held his chin in pain. Capitão do Mato walked majestically to the center of the semicircle and began to speak:

Capitao: "This is your last chance to tell us where the diamonds are hidden. If you do, your life shall be spared. But if not, then be ready to join your ancestors. We are at the right place; the journey beyond starts here. You have to choose now and here: Do you want to live or die?"

This question echoed loudly in the darkness, as powerful and eloquent as a roaring lion in the middle of the jungle.

The satellite phone rang, and Capitao do Mato picked it up after his speech. It was the General who asked to stop every execution and wait, as he was on his way to the cemetery.

During all this, Adiang confided to his friend later that he felt an unforeseen calmness inside his soul. He knew in a strange way that he was not going to die on this day, which was why he did not shout or fight back. Instead, he only defended himself or dodged the blows to avoid incurring more wounds.

Minutes later, the General made a majestic entry in a military jeep into the cemetery and ordered to see the faces of every one of the prisoners present, even those who were already buried and covered with soil. The process of digging and retrieving the bodies took a few minutes, and Adiang, along with two other gentlemen who were already in the grave, was brought out. The blood on their faces was wiped off as the General, with the help of a torch, pointed at their faces to identify each of them. While doing this, he said:

"The war is over, and we do not want any scandal. No innocent soul shall be buried here today."

It is important to mention that this was the year 2002, and the war had officially ended, although some UNITA Generals were still making their way to Luanda for the final conclusion, which occurred in 2004. The signatories to end the war were officially declared over in 2002 in Luanda, the capital city.

Upon recognizing Adiang, the General asked in shock, "What brought you here, my son?" He turned to his soldiers and shouted at them:

"Don't you know this one? Is this the man I sent you to arrest?"

A miracle had just happened, as the General recognized Adiang, who had served as a French translator in one of the transactions with French expatriates who had come into the forest to buy diamonds. Immediately, the General ordered one of his men to take Adiang to his jeep. Meanwhile, he continued to examine the corpses.

On this same day at 5 AM, accompanied by General Pai Grande, Adiang was boarding a South African Airlines flight to São Paulo, Brazil, for a new life.

On the way to the airport, Pai Grande explained to Adiang the rules of the game and the art of war. In fact, he had given too much power into the hands of his men, and with the end of the war, he had to rectify things. If not, he and everyone on his team could end up in jail. Thanks to President Jose Eduardo Dos Santos, who promised not to arrest or jail any ex-military officials, there would be no war criminals as mentioned in the peace treaty. They would live together and forgive each other for the past to build a new Angola.

Pai Grande regretted giving too much power to his men, and now was the time to deescalate that power. However, it had to be done systematically and with plenty of wisdom, as he could lose his own life in the process due to the greed of most of his men. Additionally, Pai Grande had discovered that the diamonds had never gone missing; they had been sold to his American partners, and the money was not presented to him, as Capitao do Mato and his friends had decided to keep it for themselves. This was the reason why Pai Grande came to the cemetery that night, as he didn't want innocent souls to die. Luckily for Adiang and the rest of the men, Pai Grande saved their lives.

> Remember this the next time someone tries to discourage you from pursuing your dreams: Bees don't waste their time explaining to flies why honey is better than shit..

— Nyanti

12

The Long Road to Recovery

All started at Hoji Ya Henda business centers and the Roque market in Luanda. Adiang arrived in Luanda from Lunda with the help of Moto na Ngai, who had friends and relatives in Luanda. A few days after arriving in Luanda, Adiang was connected to start giving English language classes to the kids in the neighborhood whose parents could afford it. He also worked with some West African stores as a salesman. With the almost nonexistent and precarious medical system in those days in Luanda, Adiang had no rights to any post-war trauma treatment because there would be no therapy and psychiatric follow-up.

An extremely dusty and semi-tarred road leads to the Hoji ya Henda and Roque Imbondeiro market square. This vast expanse of flat land is filled with tattered houses, shades, and warehouses constructed without any town planning, organized only in terms of tax collection, and very disorganized in other aspects, as a market should be. Hoji ya Henda and Roque markets are referential and the biggest market centers for all needs in Luanda. Slowly but steadily, Adiang has immersed himself in the commercial lifestyle in Luanda. With his jovial ability to create friendships through conversations, Adiang is a happy errand boy for most of the Malian, Senegalese, and Guinean stores that deal in housing materials, building and construction materials, and motorcycle spare parts, owned mostly by Nigerians.

The market opens at 4 AM every morning from Monday to Friday, and by 12 noon, there's no walking space as the population and merchandise occupy even the few spaces reserved for walking and transportation of goods. One has to walk through the populated market to carry goods and merchandise to the main road to catch a cab to the city, as the market is located on the outskirts of Luanda, on the road to Cacuacu, bordering Bengo Caxito. By the end of the day, typically around 6 PM or 7 PM, Adiang is exhausted and falls asleep on the floor on a mat offered to him by his friend's aunt, where he sleeps in their living room. Aunty Mado's house is a 2-bedroom block house located in Bairro Popular. The occupants are Aunty Mado and her husband, who sleep in one of the rooms, while the other room is occupied by her 4 kids, ranging from 13, 9, 7, and 5 years of age. The unique toilet for everyone is a few steps away from the house.

Adiang worked hard and doubled his earnings to get himself a small 4 by 4 meters square one-bedroom apartment with a window close to the roof, making it look like a former warehouse or night vigil room. Here, he could afford a mattress on the floor and get some good rest whenever he needed. At his former host's place, he could only come home to sleep at night, waiting until everyone was asleep to extend his mat on the floor. He was always the first to get up early in the morning so he wouldn't get in the way of the other house occupants on their way to their morning duties or to take a bath. There was no time to think about what happened in the forest during the war, except sometimes he woke up from the middle of a nightmare and realized he was inside a house, which reminded him that he was no longer in the war but in a safe place.

Adiang begins to see the importance of viewing life as a blessing and he thanks God in a different way for each day he wakes up, realizing it's a new opportunity to become somebody. To him, this is a second chance God has given him to live, and he promises himself in his daily morning prayers not to take this opportunity for granted.

Aunty Mado, a slim and tall black lady apparently in her early 40s, was not only a mother but also a wonderful Christian therapist. A fervent believer and prayer warrior, she would be the first to wake everyone for morning devotion and sing Christian songs in Lingala with such an angelic voice that it dispelled all sleepiness in the early mornings. Maybe because of her past history, she too came to Luanda after the war in the former Zaire of President Mobutu. She understood Adiang so well that she insisted on getting him a paid job as an English language teacher for the wealthy parents and their children in the neighborhood and in her church.

Aunty Mado always made time for conversation and even initiated them sometimes. Perhaps she also needed to talk about her traumas because she had fled from war to live in Luanda, or maybe she knew Adiang needed to talk about his experiences to heal. It helped in many ways to contribute to Adiang's healing, as he had someone to confide in during his dark days and someone to remind him that there was light at the end of the tunnel, and he just had to accept that light in his life. Aunty Mado always said, "There's hope, my son, believe me, there's hope. Your healing is in your perception of who you are in the Lord."

Despite her generosity and faith in God, Aunty Mado would often question how difficult it was to believe that Congo was the richest country in the world in terms of its mineral resources, yet it had the poorest living conditions for its people, marking a very drastic and frustrating reality for the country.

Embracing Freedom and Gratitude

The emotional and physical wounds acquired during the conflict were buried at the bottom of his mind, as Adiang could not afford the cost of the damages it would bring by reminding himself of the war. He decided to push all those memories to the back of his mind and focus on his newly acquired freedom and the prospect of becoming the person that had driven him to embark on this unknown journey.

With the exception of Aunty Mado, who occasionally shared her own traumas from the Congolese war, drawing parallels with biblical figures like Joseph, Moses, and even Christ himself, Adiang rarely discussed the war. Instead, she helped him see life in a different light, often saying, "Through prayers, all things are possible... Look at me, I came here almost naked with nothing, just me and the kids. Now look at us, living in this beautiful neighborhood, a beautiful house, and surrounded by beautiful people. Is there anything else you could ask from God?"

It's incredible how people living in challenging circumstances can find solace and be profoundly thankful to God. Even when their lives are precarious, their ability to express gratitude for what they have today serves as a powerful reminder of the importance of being thankful. Adiang deeply understood Aunty Mado's love and gratitude for God, knowing that she had come a long way to be where she was, and there was every reason to be grateful and to express that gratitude wholeheartedly.

Luanda at this time was far from being a peaceful city, with constant police patrols blaring sirens as arrests occurred regularly. Neighborhoods like Sambizanga, Cazenga, and Casekel were considered no-go areas, to the extent that even the police had to enter them with extreme caution due to the high prevalence of criminals and drug dealers. Walking the streets posed significant risks, as one could be arrested and even killed for minor infractions. All of these factors contributed to

Adiang's strong desire to leave the country. However, he faced a major obstacle: the cost of airfare was beyond his means. Luanda had become an extremely insecure place, with daily increases in the death toll and a surge in killings related to post-war disputes. Adiang recognized that he needed to leave in order to pursue the dream that had compelled him to leave his homeland.

> Patience: Every time you can't wait for Isaac, you'll give birth to Ishmael or something that will oppose Isaac when he arrives. Be patient with God as He shapes you. Allow the patience of God's Word to manifest in your life.
>
> *– Nyanti*

13

A New Beginning in Brazil

The South African Airlines Boeing 747 touched down on the tarmac at Guarulhos International Airport in São Paulo on a scorching afternoon. As the crew disembarked from the plane, Adiang quickly noticed that the Portuguese spoken here had some slight differences from the variety he had mastered and become accustomed to in Angola. It was clear that he would need to adapt and make some changes to ensure he could be understood in this new environment.

Undoubtedly, the airport itself was vast and beautiful, and the service provided by airport agents was outstanding. Passengers were guided by these agents and clear signboards that directed them to shuttle services for various destinations. The well-ventilated and air-conditioned airport, along with comfortable shuttle seating, provided a warm welcome to São Paulo.

Upon stepping outside the airport, Adiang was immediately hit by the heat. He wasted no time and hailed a taxi to take him to downtown São Paulo, where he had been told that Africans gathered regularly.

After checking into his hotel room and resting for a few hours, Adiang decided to explore the area in search of African restaurants for authentic African cuisine. To his surprise, he found several of them in the São Joao and Republica areas. These restaurants were predominantly Nigerian-owned and operated. The junction between São Joao and Ipiranga, which had a rich historic past, was one of the most renowned spots in the city, as celebrated by the famous Brazilian Tropicalia singer, Caetano Veloso.

Rebuilding life in Brazil presented numerous challenges, as anyone in a foreign land would encounter. However, Adiang understood that he had no alternative but to pursue further studies if he wanted to succeed in this new world and fulfill his childhood dreams.

Originally, South Africa had been his goal, but due to the circumstances he faced, Adiang had no choice but to follow the instructions of the man who had sponsored his trip to Brazil.

After the war, Adiang had spent an additional two years living in Luanda, struggling to make ends meet. He could barely afford his basic necessities, but he clung to his dreams, hoping for a miracle. That miracle did come, almost taking his life in the process, if not for the timely intervention of General Pai Grande, who rescued him from a perilous situation at a cemetery where he was meant to be executed and buried. The general had paid for Adiang's flight to Brazil, marking one of the most remarkable escapes he had ever experienced, and he was profoundly grateful.

Soon after, Adiang discovered that he was living in close proximity to one of South America's largest public hospitals, Hospital Santa Casa. He began seeking medical treatment for the war wounds he had sustained. In addition, the school located not far from his residence played a significant role in shaping his new aspirations.

In 2005, Adiang and his friends moved to the Mooca neighborhood in Sao Paulo, securing an affordable apartment with four bedrooms. Life in this new environment was simple, marked by early mornings in search of employment. However, given the precariousness of the job market, finding work was far from guaranteed, especially considering the language barrier and the challenges posed by being black and a foreigner. Unfortunately, Brazil had its share of racial discrimination, affecting equitable opportunities.

After a few months of struggling with sporadic jobs, Adiang made the decision to reenter the business world. He focused on the Angolans who dominated the trade business in Brazilian jeans and clothing, exporting them to Angola. Braz, the international commercial center, was where people of various nationalities, especially Angolans who owned many clothing shops and export companies, could be found. Adiang put his plans into action, gradually amassing a considerable income.

Within a few years, he joined forces with Nigerians to travel to neighboring Paraguay, where they purchased various goods to bring back to Brazil and sell at a significant profit. This business was commonly referred to as Brazilian "Muamba" because the goods were smuggled into the country without being declared to avoid heavy import taxes. However, this risky business came with consequences, as being caught meant losing everything and starting anew. They also had to navigate through challenging routes, sometimes through insecure roads without police control, and faced the risk of bandits confiscating their goods or resorting to violence for money.

In 2006, Adiang's tireless efforts culminated in a career change and training that ultimately turned him into a celebrated artist in Brazil.

To pursue this new dream, Adiang continued to draw inspiration from the words of Nyanti, "Education is the key," as he enrolled in the School of Dramatic Arts and Television (Teatro Escola Macunaima), located in Santa Cecilia, close to the first house he lived in upon arriving in Brazil.

During his time in jail at the Comarca Central Prison in Angola, telenovelas were the only form of entertainment that prisoners were passionate about. The storyline, drama, language, and lifestyle depicted in these shows reflected the lives of Portuguese-speaking countries in Africa. Every Angolan prisoner aspired to dress, look, and speak like the characters in Brazilian novelas. This profound influence had a lasting impact on Adiang's aspirations, and he made a solemn promise to himself that one day he would appear on these TV shows.

Adiang's determination to achieve greatness surpassed the regret he felt for the losses, injuries, pains, and trauma he had endured during the civil war in Angola. He was resolute in keeping his promise to himself, and the opportunity had finally arrived. Nothing could deter him, not even the challenges of living in a foreign city where the language was his primary barrier. He had come too far to turn back now.

Without any formal or prior Portuguese language training, Adiang embarked on paid classes at Macunaima. He faced discouragement from some of his friends in Sao Paulo, who doubted his ability to make it on TV. However, after three years of unwavering dedication and relentless study, Adiang graduated as a professional actor.

It's worth noting that those who discourage or hate on you can, in fact, serve as a motivational force to help you achieve your dreams. Sometimes, God places such individuals in your life to remind you of the importance of your dreams and motivate you to prove them wrong. Their true purpose is to assist you in completing what you've started, what God has placed inside you. They are blessings in disguise. God often tests us in various ways to see if we truly desire what we ask of Him. Embracing life's challenges and overcoming loneliness can open doors to victory and excellence. Just like diamonds are brought from the dirt before they shine on rings in shopping centers, or gold is polished after going through the furnace and intense heat, challenges and struggles prepare you for greatness. Embrace the struggle, as it is a pathway to excellence, and remember that God prepares you before exposing you to a platform of greatness.

While still a student, Adiang actively participated in TV commercials, TV shows, and various television-related activities.

Driven by an insatiable passion, Adiang decided to take the National Board exam for admission to SP Escola de Teatro with a scholarship program to become a film and stage play director. To the astonishment of many friends who saw him making money as a student instead of paying fees, Adiang passed the exam with flying colors. Out of the two thousand students who registered for this public exam, only two hundred were granted entry, and the top one hundred received full scholarships from the government of Sao Paulo to support their education. This is how Adiang secured his spot among the first 100 students in the program at SP Escola de Teatro.

However, Adiang faced periods of financial hardship in Brazil, enduring months and even a year without employment and struggling to pay his bills. Consequently, he was evicted from his apartment, which he had been living in alone due to its proximity to his school. Times were so tough that he decided to escape to Argentina, hoping for better prospects. After spending six months in Buenos Aires, he returned to Sao Paulo, only to find himself without a place to live. His former housemate, with whom he used to share accommodation, turned him away, insisting that he couldn't stay there unless he contributed to the bills.

Adiang, who speaks four languages, is interpreting the gospel alongside Pastors Izik Maxwell and Obi Franklin.

With no other options, Adiang turned to prayer and sought refuge in his faith. He had neglected his relationship with God during his more prosperous days and had distanced himself from the church. In his pursuit of a lavish lifestyle, he had spent all his money, and his friends were nowhere to be found. Adiang found himself alone on the streets of Sao Paulo once again.

Left with no alternatives, Adiang hurried back to the famous (CCMI) Christian Community Ministry International church in Sao Paulo, which always welcomed Africans, especially Nigerians, who were struggling in Brazil. He had established valuable friendships in the past with influential church members and often collaborated with some of the pastors as an interpreter on mission trips.

Meeting Pastor John

While in church and deep in prayer, Pastor John approached Adiang, inquiring about his well-being. Adiang shared his troubles, and before he could finish explaining, Pastor John offered a solution. He asked Adiang to carry his luggage and join him, as he would be staying with him until he could find his own place. This turn of events felt like a plot from one of the telenovelas Adiang used to act in on TV. He couldn't believe his ears and sought confirmation from Pastor John, who affirmed his offer.

Living with Pastor John presented its own challenges, as there was another young man called Paul residing in one of the two-bedroom apartments near Metro Itaquera. Paul made Adiang's life miserable. Despite several attempts to kick Adiang out of the house, Pastor John refused to send Adiang away. Frustration reached a boiling point when Paul confronted Adiang, insisting that he leave because his presence was disturbing. In response, Adiang, with a wry smile, told Paul that 'a corpse is not afraid of the coffin.' Their heated argument nearly escalated into a physical altercation, but Adiang warned him that he had the right to self-defense and the means to leave Brazil, should things turn ugly. Paul retreated, grumbling.

Later that day, Pastor John intervened and resolved the dispute by reminding the young man that he was there by invitation and not responsible for any expenses. He questioned why the young man wanted to force a fellow brother out of the house. With that, peace was restored in the house.

Under Pastor John's guidance, the housemates embraced a routine of three daily prayer sessions and two days of fasting each week. Regardless of their locations, when the designated prayer times arrived, they found a place to pray alongside Pastor John over the phone. This practice, had a healing effect on them.

Three months later, Adiang began to see the fruits of their prayers as his agent contacted him, and he returned to television with even better roles. A year later, he found himself at the Actors Studio in New York City, honing his acting career.

The section concludes with a cautionary note, reminding readers to remain vigilant in their faith and to be cautious about the company they keep, as success can sometimes lead people away from their spiritual paths. The author emphasizes the need to control one's thoughts and be mindful of the devil's influence, which may come in unexpected forms, including through close friends.

Adiang's Journey to Stardom and Healing

After nearly a decade of living in Brazil, Adiang not only became a television star but also a prominent figure in the African community in Brazil. He had ventured to the United States for further studies multiple times and returned to Brazil, where his career as an actor and television personality thrived. Some of his notable contributions included appearances on sitcoms, TV series for GloboTV, HBO Latin America, GNT Globo, and numerous stage plays throughout the country, most notably the annual "Passion of Christ" live performance, which was televised nationally, as well as various TV commercials.

In 2014, Adiang received the honor of being named the Best African Actor in Brazil, and the ceremony, organized by the Government of Sao Paulo in collaboration with the African Cultural Center, was attended by his family and friends. During the same year, he decided to fulfill his dream of organizing an African Film Festival in Brazil, which he named the "KILIMANJARO FilmFest."

This event was made possible through collaborations with entities such as the French Embassy, Sao Paulo Cultural Center (SESC), Alliance Française, Institut Français, Cine France, and Fundacao da Cultura. Adiang served as the CEO, Creator, and Curator of the festival, where he showcased the socioeconomic, political, and cultural realities of Africa before and after independence. The festival featured ongoing debates that brought together people from all walks of life to confront the realities of being African in the diaspora and surviving despite numerous challenges.

Within this platform, Adiang also used cinema documentaries to shed light on the risks of drug dealing faced by many vulnerable Africans in pursuit of quick money. His films portrayed the dangers of individuals serving as drug mules who swallow drugs, later expelling them through their excrement once they reach their destination. Unfortunately, not all of them succeeded in reaching their destination, as some were apprehended and faced lengthy jail terms or experienced drug-related accidents.

The opportunity to become an actor, where Adiang could transform into various characters on stage or in movies, was not only therapeutic but also a significant source of redemption for him. While performing, he became fully immersed in the roles, losing track of time and temporarily forgetting the pain of the civil war. He remained in character even after the scenes were completed. Adiang had managed to erase and overcome his traumatic past by becoming someone else, and the stage played a pivotal role in his healing process—it was more than just therapy; it was a profound transformation.

After much hesitation, Adiang accepted an invitation in 2016 to return to Angola for a one-month acting workshop and participate in a career talk show on TV ZIMBO, where he shared insights into his life journey and his success in Brazilian TV. Adiang leverages his experiences and talent in talk shows and motivational workshops to inspire young people to overcome their challenges and discover hope within themselves. He emphasizes that everything they need is already within them, as God has created them in His image and endowed them with all the necessary qualities to be the best version of themselves.

Adiang encourages them to stop comparing themselves to others, reminding them that they are already perfect just as they are, but they must have the desire to achieve their goals. He states, "I am a singer, actor, engineer, physician, scientist, etc., because I can, not because I want. Those who merely want will continue wanting until they lead unfulfilled lives, while those who can continue to achieve, grow, and innovate because they possess the capability." Adiang concludes with an empowering message: "YES, YOU CAN—just believe it."

Adiang continues to conduct motivational workshops around the world, particularly in the USA and Africa.

> "A person is not great because they haven't failed; a person is great because failure hasn't stopped them."
>
> – *Nyanti*

14

Giving Back

The KILIMANJARO Film Festival is a pioneering platform dedicated to giving back to society. It stands apart by emphasizing education rather than focusing solely on awards. Through the medium of cinema, Adiang imparts valuable lessons, guiding individuals to navigate existential challenges and work toward the betterment of society. The festival, held annually in November, coincides with Brazil's Black History Month. During this time, KILIMANJARO warmly welcomes filmmakers, actors, actresses, and journalists from around the world and within Brazil.

In partnership with the French Embassy and Cinemateca in Brazil, KILIMANJARO secures a selection of films from renowned festivals like CANNES and FESPACO (The PANAFRICAN FilmFest) in Burkina Faso. These films are thoughtfully chosen to align with the festival's annual theme. Adiang, well-versed in the traumas and challenges faced by young people globally, particularly in Brazil and Africa, sheds light on the socioeconomic, political, and cultural hurdles they encounter.

The festival's sessions, attended by university professors, primary and secondary school teachers, parents, and everyday citizens of Sao Paulo, foster vibrant debates. These discussions yield valuable insights, contributing to the ongoing effort to create a better society. The world is composed of diverse individuals, each making their unique contributions towards improving the world for current and future generations. It is a shared responsibility to leave a legacy of progress and inspire future generations to continue building upon the foundation we lay.

Inspiring the Next Generation

Adiang's impact extends to his church, where he passionately imparts acting classes to enthusiastic children who affectionately refer to him as Uncle Tom. Their dedication is rewarded with gifts, trophies, and delectable chocolates. It's quite amusing to witness their initial frustration when Uncle Tom misses a Sunday school class, only to be charmed into peace the following Sunday with chocolates and biscuits. After that experience, Adiang has made a solemn commitment to never miss a Sunday again, understanding that these young thespians hold him accountable.

Sharing the stage with these kids is more than a blessing; it's a healing process. It serves as a poignant reminder of the opportunities they didn't have as children born in Africa in the 70s.

Adiang Assuoe

Adiang's journey is a testament to the unique paths we all tread. Each person's journey is meticulously proportioned by God, reflecting the immense grace and glory upon their lives. Some of us bear the responsibility of being a cornerstone for many, and failing to fulfill this role can have dire consequences for those who depend on us. Consider the stories of Joseph, Moses, Esther, and her Uncle Mordecai, or the narrative of Christ, who, according to Christians, sacrificed himself to save humanity.

Adiang giving a speech.

Adiang's story prompts us to ponder how prepared we are to sacrifice for a brighter future for our children. Are we willing to endure loneliness, scarcity, pain, trauma, and the absence of a loving partner to secure a better life for ourselves and our offspring?

Do not assign blame to anyone for the current situation you are facing. This is your time to labor, for the harvest season will arrive, and you must be prepared to withstand the fierce winds of adversities that seek to bring you down. Remember that God understands you better than you understand yourself.

As I pen down this true life story, I reflect on the years it took me to decide whether to share it or not. I implore you not to wait as long, for everything you need resides within you. Forge ahead and excel, for you are crafted from remarkable material. No amount of prayer and fasting alone will elevate you to your desired platform of excellence. You must also take decisive action and hold a profound reverence for God in your life.

"It's within you, Everything you need in life, Is wrapped up in the Word. Once you grasp it, Keep speaking it, Never cease proclaiming it. As the Bible declares, 'So mightily grew the word of God and prevailed.' I have discovered the path I must follow In the name of Jesus, The Lord is my Shepherd, I shall not want. He makes me lie down in green pastures, He leads me beside the still waters, He restores my soul, He guides me in the path of righteousness for His name's sake... Amen. Yeah, Pastor Chris Oyakilome... worth hearing.

Like my mum would say…

> Son, never play the same game as them. They count on their families, but your family counts on you. Be very careful. Remember that one day these friends will all go away, and you'll be left alone. The situation at home will remain the same if you forget what family you come from, what type of life your family lives. There are those who succeed with the help of their parents, but you will have to succeed to help your family. You are not fighting the same fight. They were born on the right side of the shore, but you have to throw yourself into the river and face the crocodiles to succeed. Be very careful, son.

— Nyanti

About the Author

Adiang Assuoe is a multi-talented filmmaker, journalist, and actor hailing from Cameroon, whose journey through the worlds of sports commentary, theater, and cinema has taken him from the vibrant streets of Cameroon to the bustling cities of Brazil and the United States. Born and raised in Cameroon, Adiang's passion for storytelling and performance found its roots early in life.

Adiang began his career as a radio sports commentator and analyst for Cameroon Foot Pools, lending his voice to the excitement and drama of the beautiful game on FM Mount Cameroon and Radio Buea. However, his artistic pursuits soon led him on a global odyssey of learning and self-discovery.

In Brazil, Adiang pursued his love for the arts, earning a diploma in Acting from the prestigious Teatro Escola Macunaima and Incenna Escola de TV e Cinema. He further honed his skills by obtaining a diploma in stage play direction from SP Escola de Teatro and a certification in special effects in cinema from Universidade Anhembi Morumbi, both located in Brazil.

Adiang's quest for artistic excellence took him to the heart of the entertainment world, where he earned a Diploma in Acting from the renowned Actors Studio in New York City,

USA. This experience provided him with invaluable insights into the craft and the opportunity to collaborate with some of the industry's finest talents.

Throughout his illustrious career, Adiang has left an indelible mark on the entertainment industry. His acting prowess has graced various mediums, including television commercials, TV series, films, and stage plays in Brazil and South America. He is widely recognized for his lead roles in the acclaimed Globotv series "O CAÇADOR" and the HBO Latin America series "DESTINOSP." Notably, he shared the screen with legendary world champion Mike Tyson in a Skol beer commercial in Brazil and portrayed Simon of Cyrene in the televised open-air stage play "THE PASSION OF CHRIST."

Adiang's talent and dedication have not gone unnoticed, earning him the title of Best Actor at the Afro-Brazil Awards in 2014. In addition to his acting career, Adiang is a prolific filmmaker, with a remarkable documentary titled *"Digging for Life"* to his credit, which has garnered numerous awards at various film festivals around the world.

Beyond his artistic endeavors, Adiang is a creator and curator, responsible for establishing the African Film Festival in Brazil, known as the KILIMANJARO Film Festival, and serving as the curator of the Brazilian International Film Festival, Festcimm. He is also a versatile communicator, having achieved a certification in Broadcast Journalism from the New York Film Academy.

Adiang is not only an artist but also a public motivational speaker, sharing his insights and experiences in humanitarian NGOs, schools, universities, churches, homeless shelters, and various other platforms. He is a master of ceremonies, lending his charismatic presence to diverse events.

In his leisure time, Adiang indulges in a range of hobbies, including soccer, reading, tourism, tennis, swimming, movies, listening to music, engaging in mind-sharpening activities, and public speaking.

With a command of multiple languages, including English, Spanish, Portuguese, and French, Adiang Assuoe's artistic journey continues to transcend borders and cultures, captivating audiences worldwide. He currently divides his time between São Paulo, Brazil, and New York City, USA, leaving an indomitable imprint on the global entertainment landscape.

To get in touch or for more information please visit:

www.AdiangAssuoe.com

kama.dc and **thenigeriancenter**
Martin Luther King Jr. Memorial Library

KAMA DC Storytelling Night:

IMMIGRANTS CELEBRATING INDEPENDENCE & INDIVIDUALITY

Tommy Germain

Tommy is a filmmaker, journalist, and actor, born and raised in Cameroon. He produced an award-winning documentary based on his true life experience during the Angolan civil war. He's also worked as a television presenter, singer, and dancer, and even acted in commercials with champion boxer Mike Tyson.

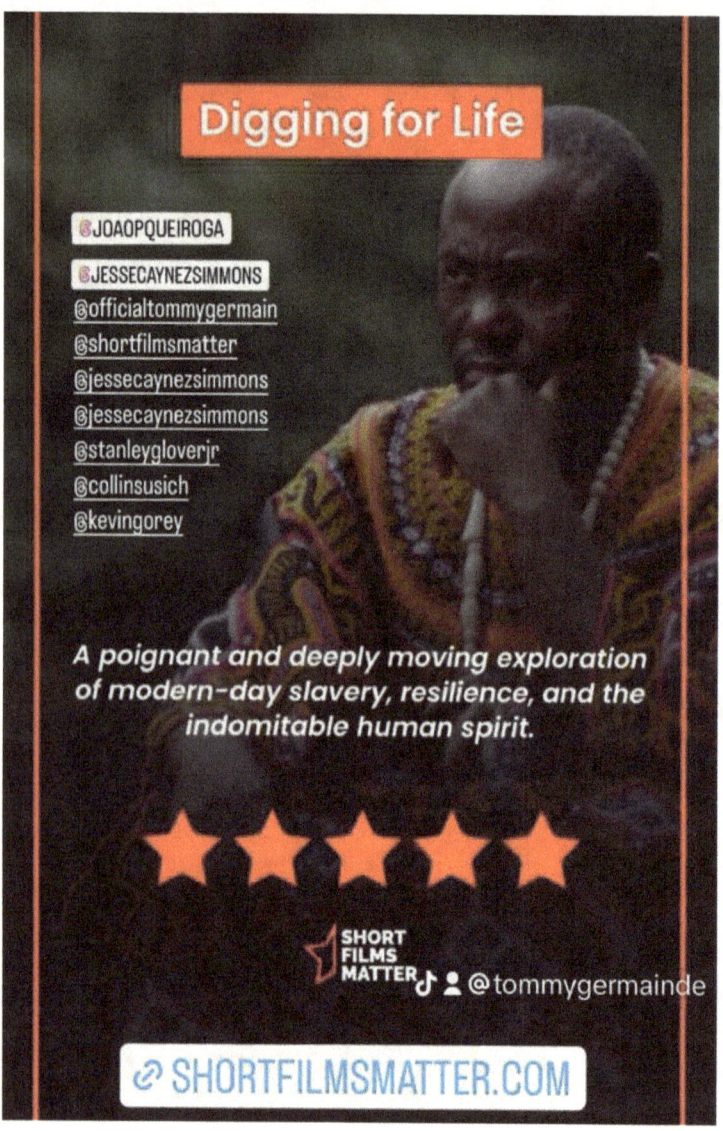

www.ingramcontent.com/pod-product-compliance
Lightning Source LLC
Chambersburg PA
CBHW052056110526
44591CB00013B/2238